SWITCHBLADE HONEY

WARREN ELLIS
BRANDON McKINNEY

AiT/PLANETLAR
SAN FRANCISCO

Switchblade Honey
By Warren Ellis and Brandon McKinney

Published by
AiT/Planet Lar
2034 47th Avenue
San Francisco, CA 94116

first edition: July 2003
second edition: February 2004

10 9 8 7 6 5 4 3 2

Copyright © 2003 Warren Ellis.   All rights reserved.

Cover illustration by Brandon McKinney
Cover design by Brian Wood
Book design by Whiskey Island
Lettered by Ryan Yount

ISBN: 1-932051-13-9

Printed and bound in Canada by Quebecor Printing, Inc.

SWITCHBLADE HONEY

INTRODUCTION

Like so many things in my life, it started out as a bad joke.

My girlfriend Niki will not thank me for revealing this, but during the first year or so of our daughter's life, she became a *Star Trek* viewer. Her story is that Lili would fall asleep on her, thereby pinning her down, at the same time every day – when *Star Trek: The Next Generation* came on. And, I dunno, she couldn't reach the zapper or her eyelids fused into the top of her head or something and she had to watch them all.

So, every now and then, we take a quick look at whatever new iteration of *Star Trek* is on. Mostly so I can take the piss out of her mercilessly. There we are one evening, taking in ten minutes of an awful, pompous, stupid thing called *Star Trek: Voyager.* It features an actress who chooses to essay, if you can imagine, Katherine Hepburn impersonating William Shatner. It is uniquely horrible.

And we're watching this, and making idle comments that our friend Patrick Stewart is really much better (once again glossing over the time when Patrick phoned and Niki refused to believe it was him, insisting that it was one of my friends doing a funny voice to fuck with us) and they should have gotten someone like him, because frankly if you don't have an actor of his strength anchoring the thing then you may as well go home, and all that, and then I have what is to me suddenly the most entertaining thought.

"They should get Ray Winstone as captain."

Ray Winstone is an excellent British actor who tends to play working-class London psychotics. Even when he's the good guy – he was Will Scarlet in a long-running Robin Hood TV show here, and portrayed a hero journalist type in *Tank Malling* – he's usually fucking terrifying. Only once in (my) recent memory has he played against type in film, as the scared safecracker in *Sexy Beast.* See, everyone first saw Ray Winstone as a teenager whipping other kids to death with a pool ball in a sock, screaming WHO'S THE DADDY NOW? WHO'S THE FUCKING DADDY NOW? I'M THE DADDY NOW! He's a force of nature, a thing driven by beer and cigarettes and kicking fucking heads in. He's got a chubby face and little boy's eyes that, in the moment, go black and dead like shark's eyes. Reduces London English to a series of grunts and yelps. He is, in fact, The Greatest Living Londoner.

And the whole thing unfurled as I spoke, like a flag that someone had wiped their arse on first. Insisting on smoking on the bridge. Ray Winstone has to have his fags (which in Britain means "cigarettes" – it's the first term we purge from our vocabulary when we travel to America). And beer. "Have one of our futuristic blue drinks with no alcohol, sir?" "Fuck off. Fucking *pint*, son. Right fucking now." That standard *Star Trek* moment when someone asks the captain if they can go now, and spouts some techno bollocks at him about how the course is set and all that. "Well, fucking *go on then*, son. Twat."

Ray Winstone, in one of his usual character types, as the captain of a spaceship. It was funny for a minute. We moved on.

A day later, story elements started occurring to me.

There was a lot of running around shouting "No, get out of my brain" and drinking of whiskey and firing flare guns up my nose and things.

None of which did a blind bit of good, of course. You have to give in to the ideas when they come. Somehow, this vision of Ray Winstone saying "Bollocks" in space had triggered some creative gag reflex, and all my loathing of that profoundly ordinary, polite, self-important and bland future presented by TV science-fiction came surging up. All yellow, and with bits in.

I'm not the only one this has ever happened to, of course. There's a lovely bit in Spider and Jeanne Robinson's novel *Stardance* where the two protagonists of the latter part of the book are taken aboard a military spaceship and given cigarettes and wrist-worn air-scrubbing fans to suck away the smoke. (The same authors who taught an impressionable young man that you have to keep sucking on your joint during dinner because eating takes the edge off your buzz.) These were people who were serious about their vices and did not see science fiction as a way to whitewash out everything that is fun about self-destructive habits and being human.

(Incidentally, I did indeed start smoking again around the time I was finishing this book. I'm going to quit again some time this year, although life keeps conspiring against me. I'm pretty sure I'm genetically hardwired for nicotine input, but it smells bad. It's no wonder people battling with cigarettes kept turning up in my work of the last couple of years. I may switch to heroin.)

I present to you, then, a joke. An extended gag at the expense of the colourless, clean SF of the big media. The anti-*Star Trek*, if you like. Almost automatic writing; a joke told in my voice, full of my usual rubbish. I think it's a good joke, and worth the time it takes to tell it to you, otherwise it wouldn't be here and neither would I.

I'm just saying, be advised. This isn't me at my most blisteringly intellectual. SWITCHBLADE HONEY is, in fact, me drunk and wreathed in fag smoke (shut up) and having a laugh with my girlfriend.

Thank God Brandon McKinney was sober, eh?

Warren Ellis
Middle of the night, too pissed to see the clock
Fucking England, innit

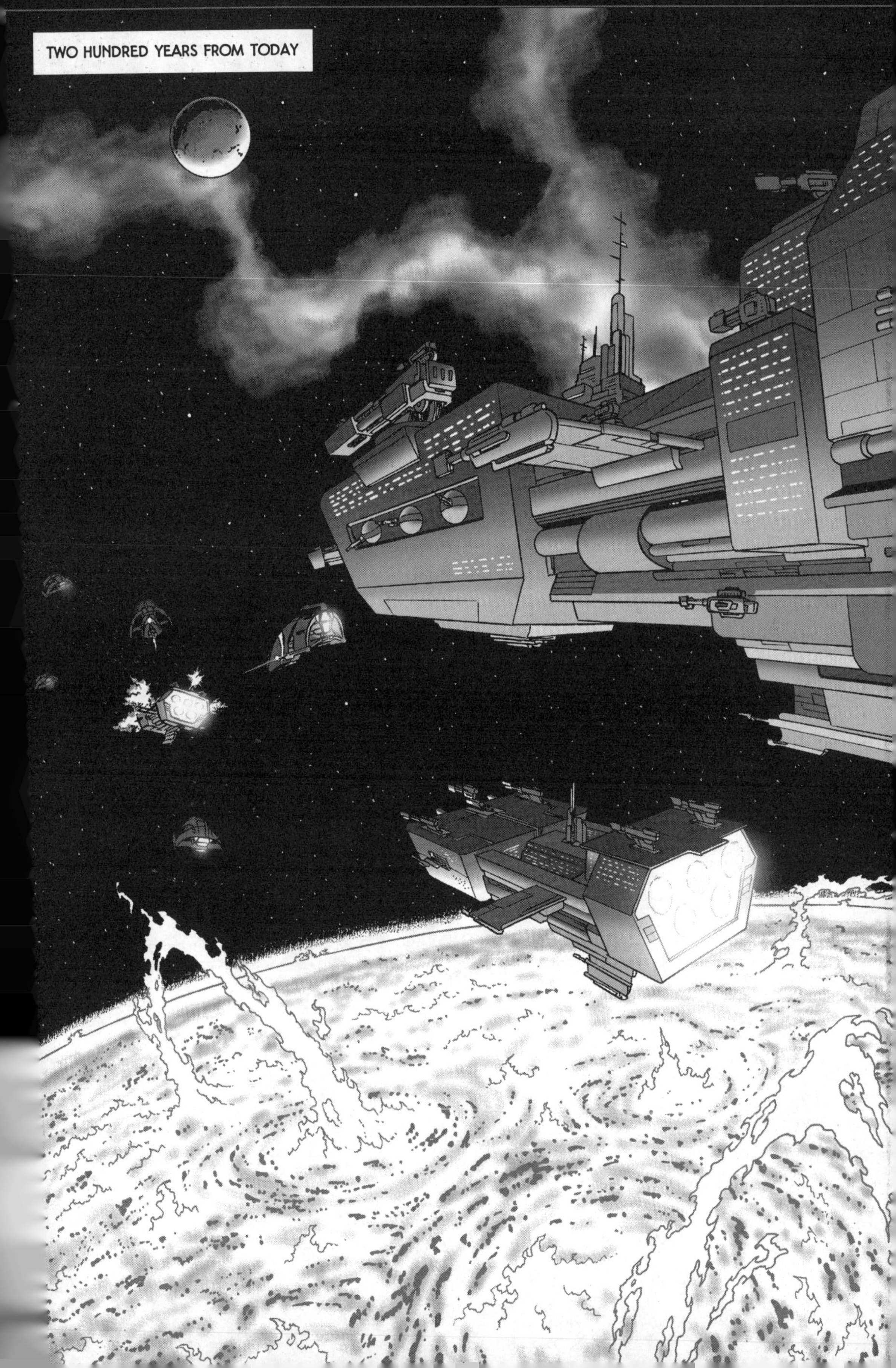
TWO HUNDRED YEARS FROM TODAY

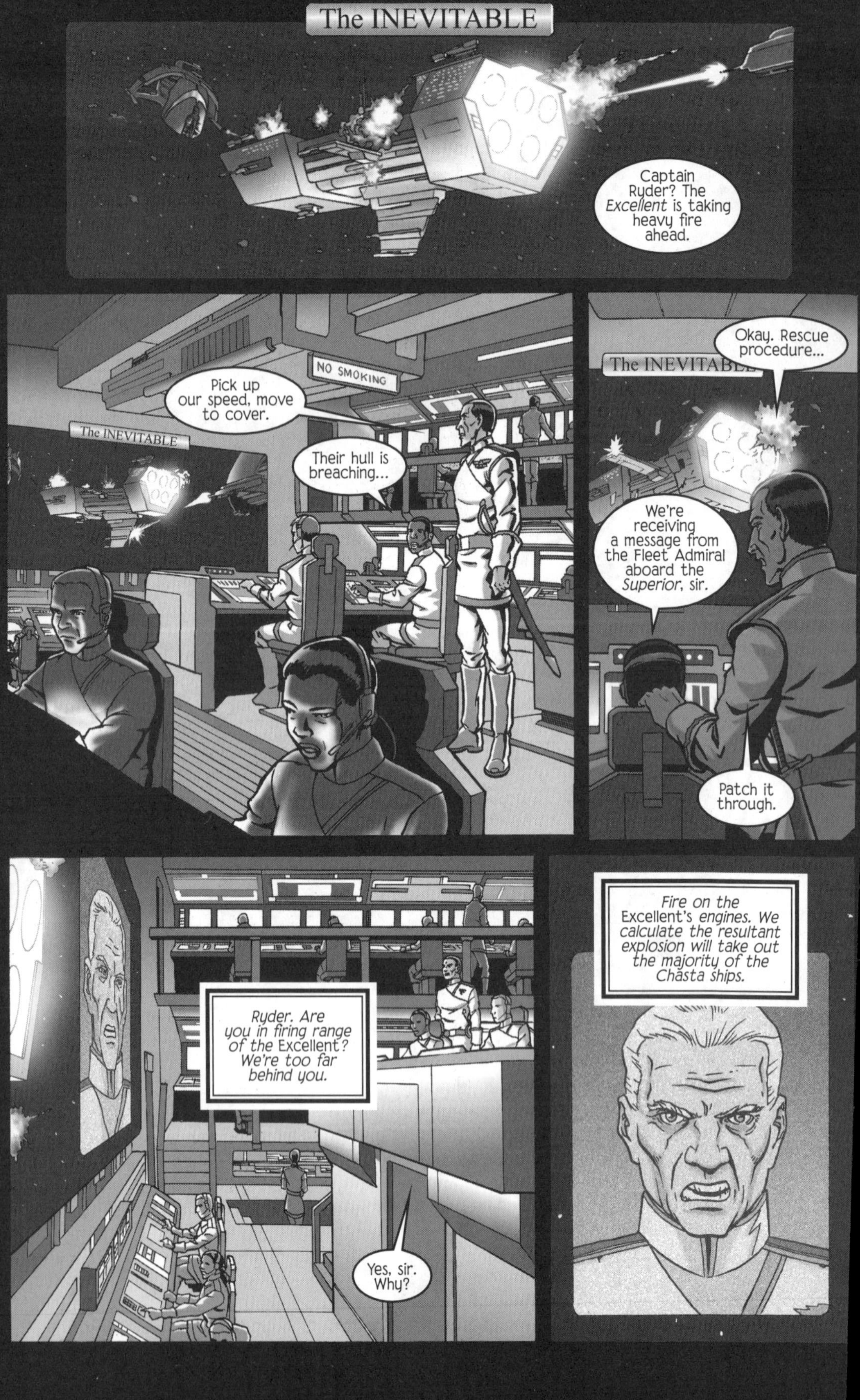

The INEVITABLE
Captain Ryder? The Excellent is taking heavy fire ahead.
NO SMOKING
Pick up our speed, move to cover.
The INEVITABLE
Their hull is breaching...
Okay. Rescue procedure...
We're receiving a message from the Fleet Admiral aboard the Superior, sir.
Patch it through.
Ryder. Are you in firing range of the Excellent? We're too far behind you.
Yes, sir. Why?
Fire on the Excellent's engines. We calculate the resultant explosion will take out the majority of the Chasta ships.

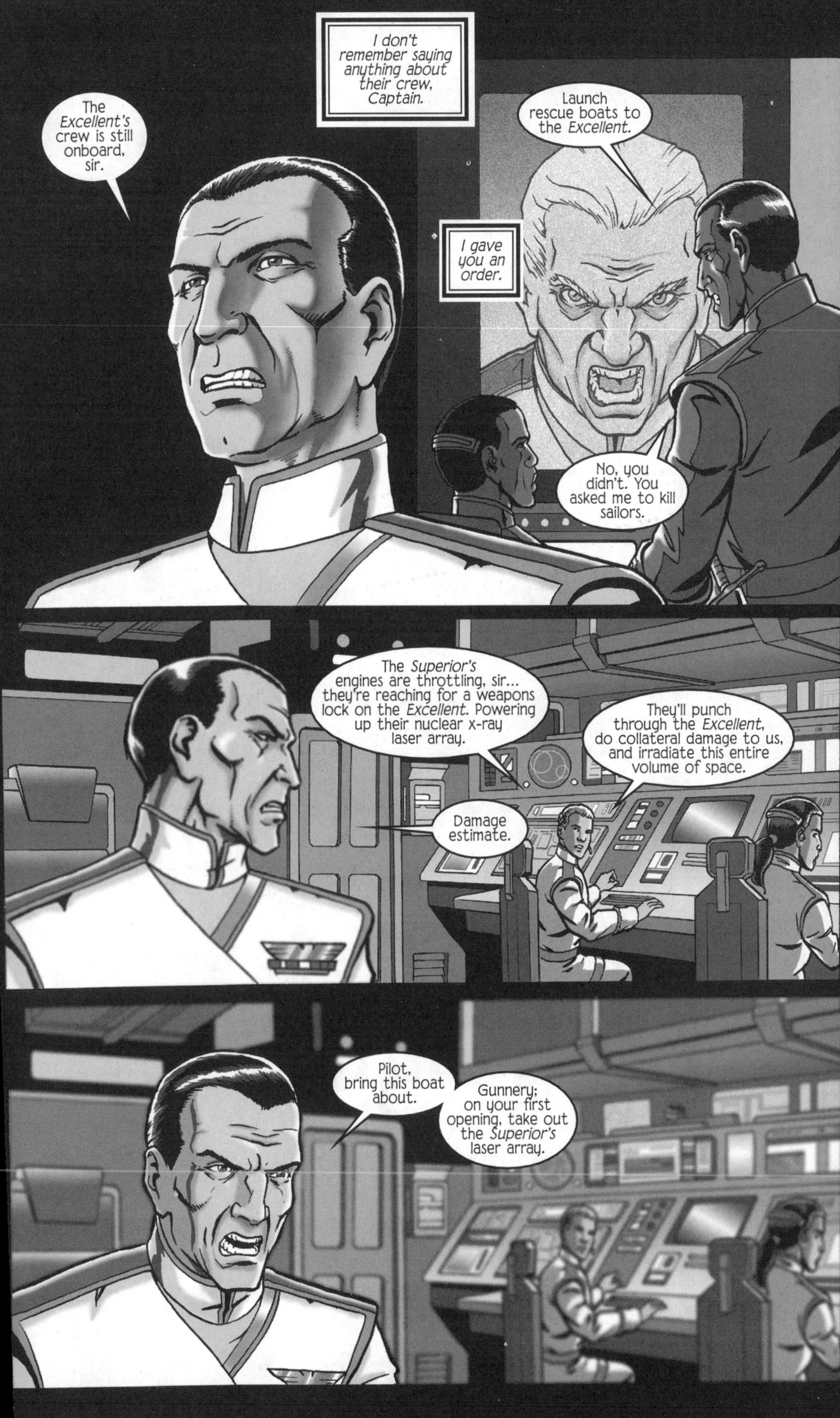
I don't remember saying anything about their crew, Captain.
The *Excellent's* crew is still onboard, sir.
Launch rescue boats to the *Excellent*.
I gave you an order.
No, you didn't. You asked me to kill sailors.
The *Superior's* engines are throttling, sir... they're reaching for a weapons lock on the *Excellent*. Powering up their nuclear x-ray laser array.
Damage estimate.
They'll punch through the *Excellent*, do collateral damage to us, and irradiate this entire volume of space.
Pilot, bring this boat about.
Gunnery; on your first opening, take out the *Superior's* laser array.

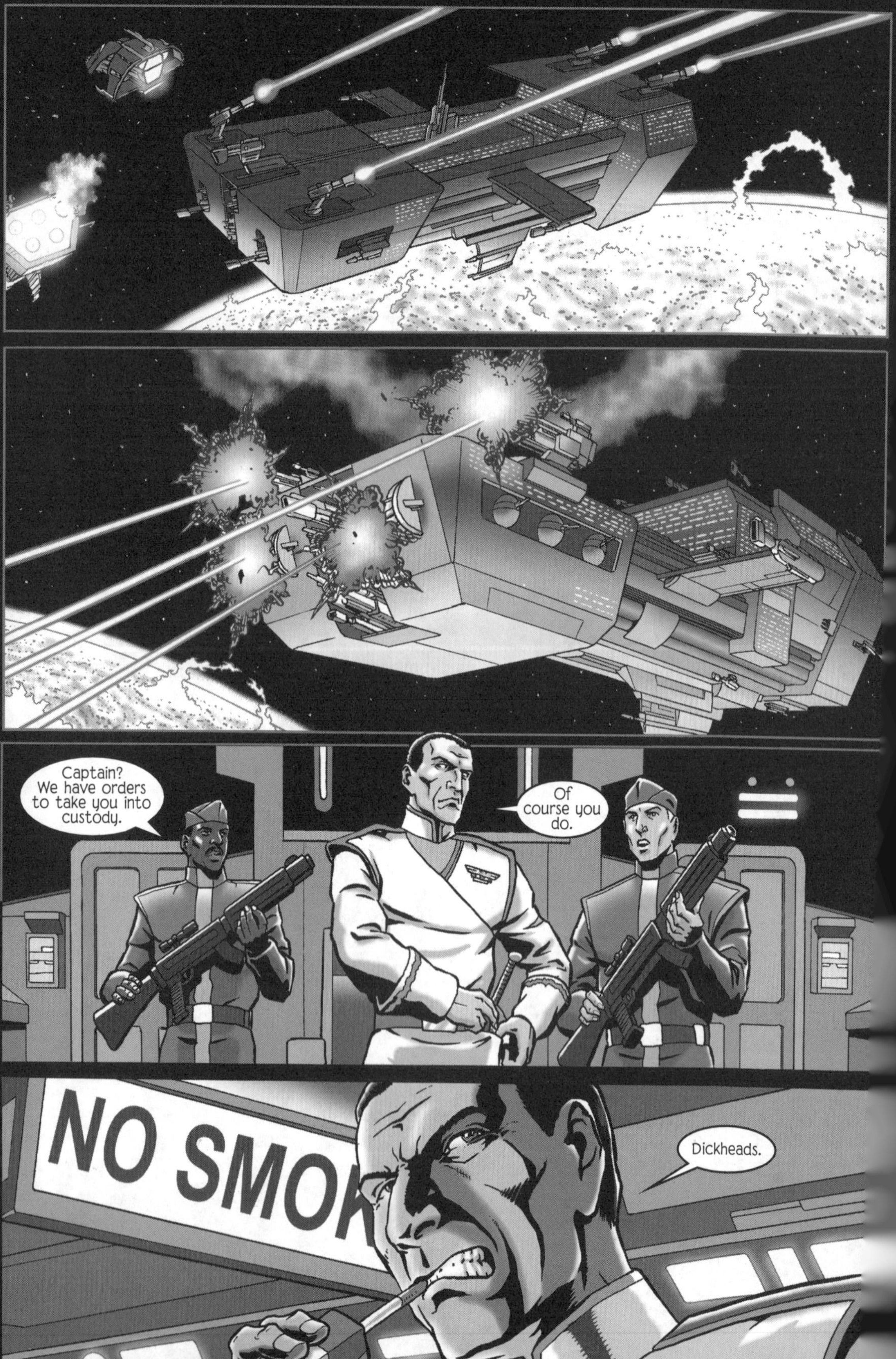
Captain? We have orders to take you into custody.
Of course you do.
NO SMOK
Dickheads.

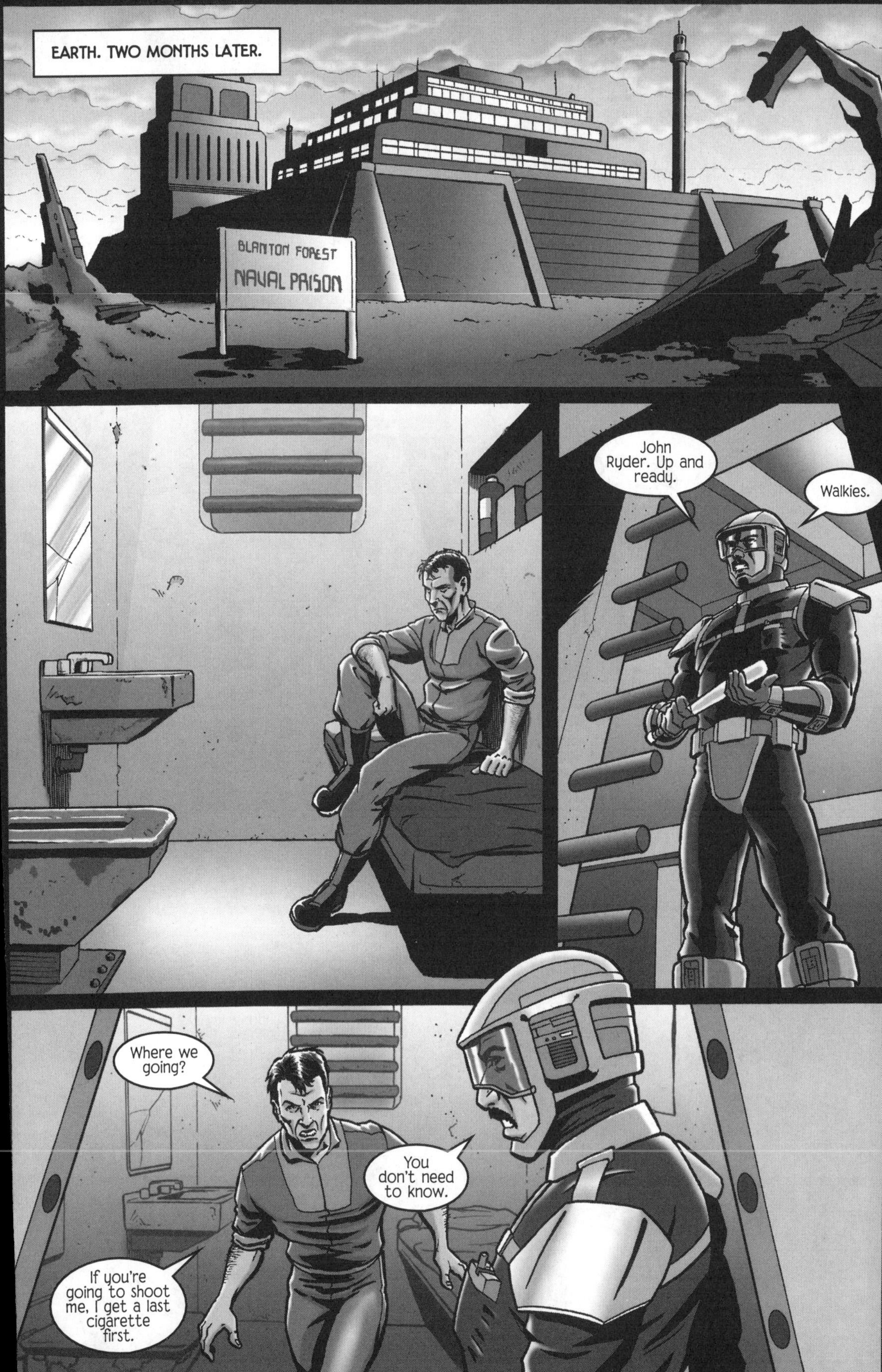
EARTH. TWO MONTHS LATER.
BLANTON FOREST
NAVAL PRISON
John Ryder. Up and ready.
Walkies.
Where we going?
You don't need to know.
If you're going to shoot me, I get a last cigarette first.

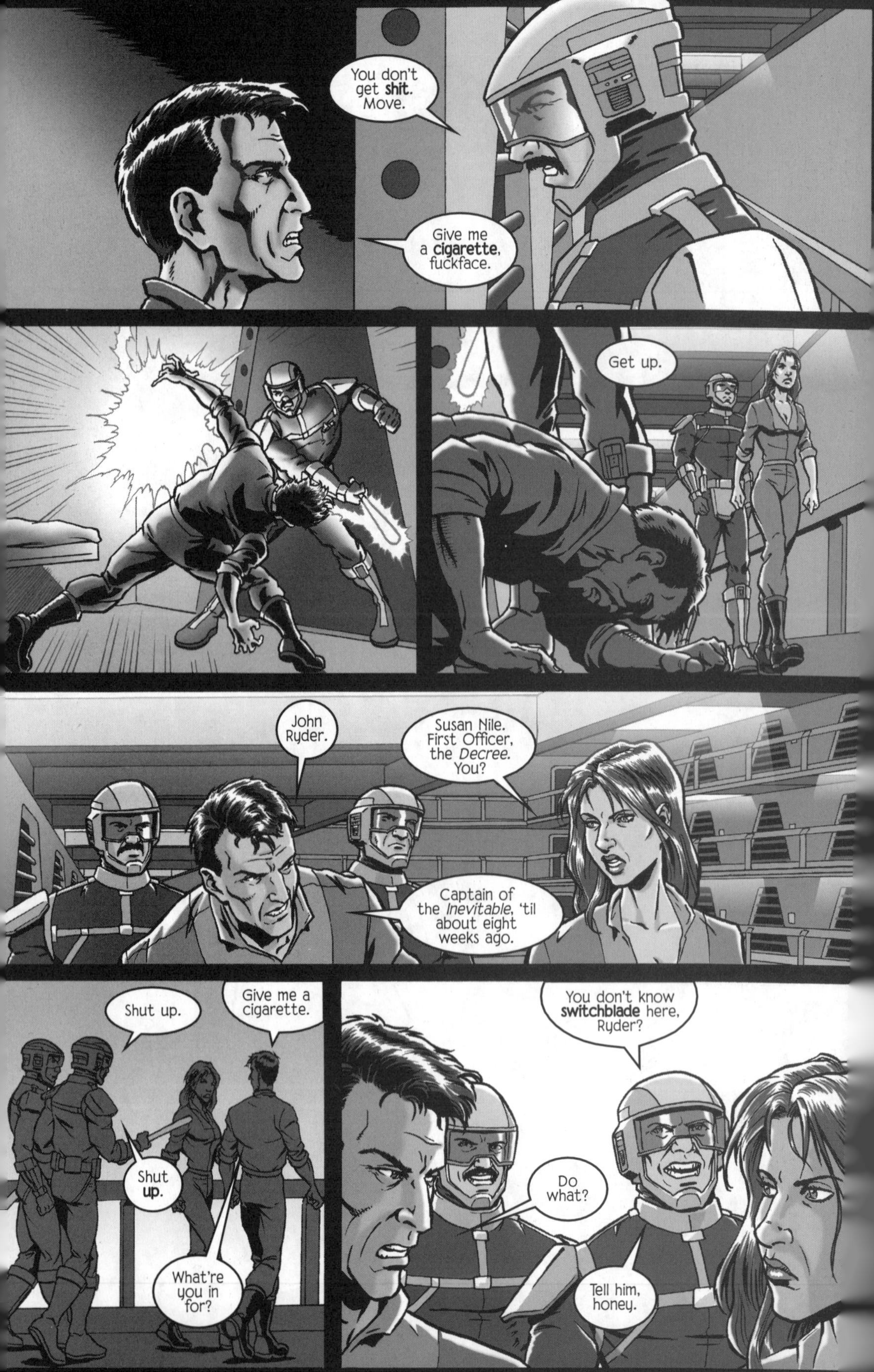
Give me a **cigarette**, fuckface.
You don't get **shit**. Move.
Get up.
John Ryder.
Susan Nile. First Officer, the *Decree*. You?
Captain of the *Inevitable*, 'til about eight weeks ago.
Give me a cigarette.
Shut up.
Shut **up**.
What're you in for?
You don't know **switchblade** here, Ryder?
Do what?
Tell him, honey.

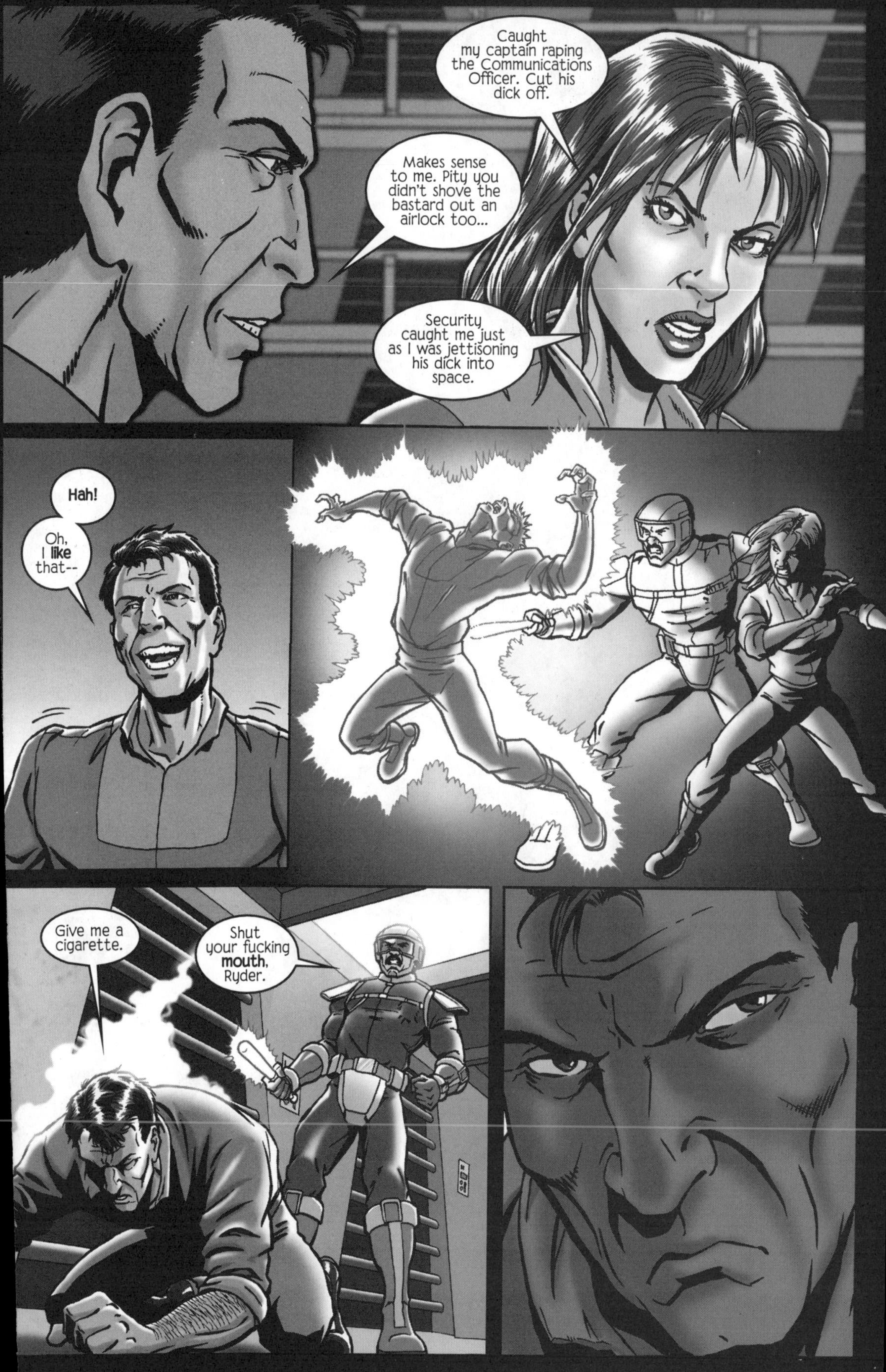
Caught my captain raping the Communications Officer. Cut his dick off.
Makes sense to me. Pity you didn't shove the bastard out an airlock too...
Security caught me just as I was jettisoning his dick into space.
Hah!
Oh, I **like** that--
Give me a cigarette.
Shut your fucking **mouth,** Ryder.

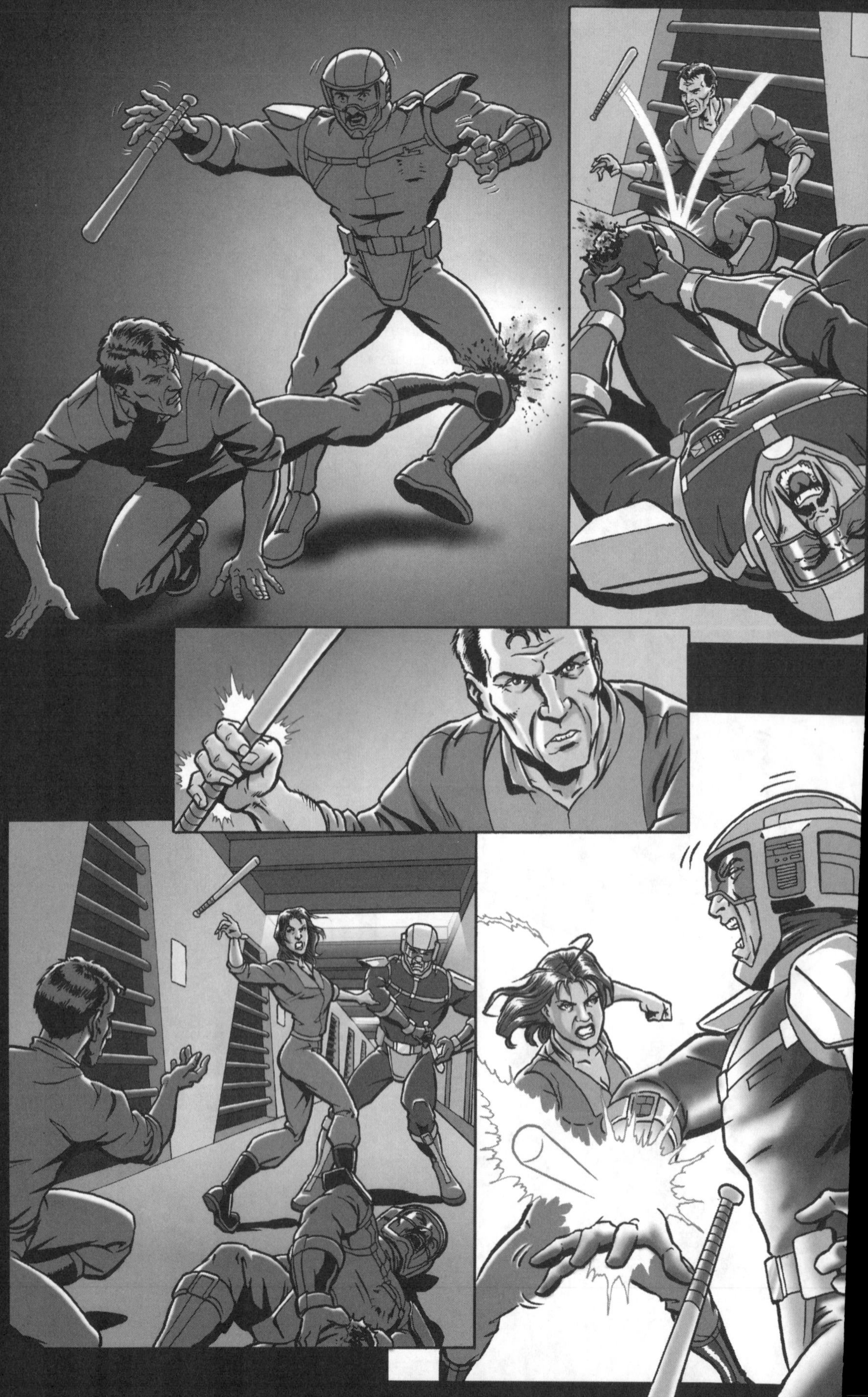

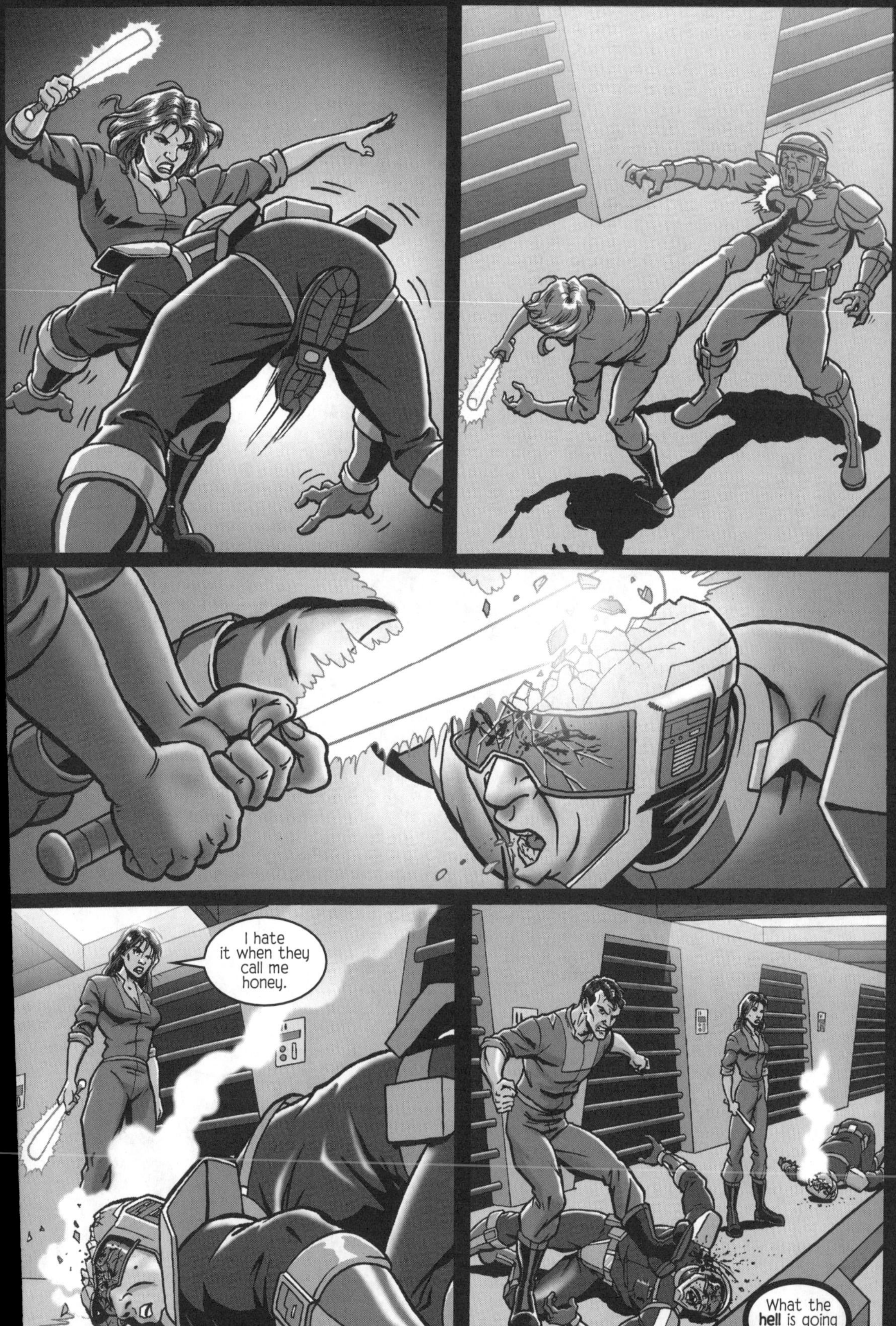
I hate
it when they
call me
honey.
What the
hell is going
on here?

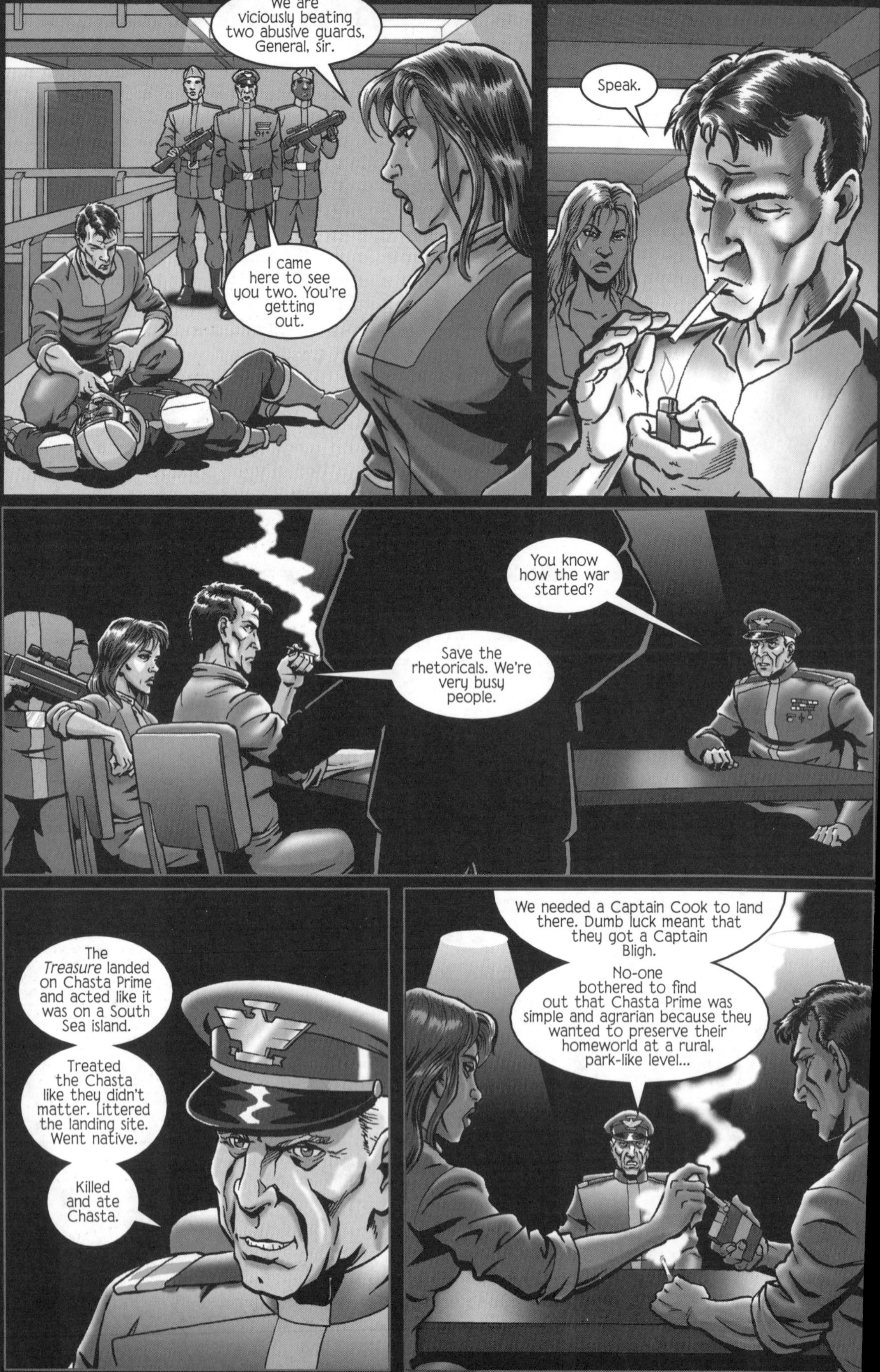
We are viciously beating two abusive guards, General, sir.
I came here to see you two. You're getting out.
Speak.
You know how the war started?
Save the rhetoricals. We're very busy people.
The *Treasure* landed on Chasta Prime and acted like it was on a South Sea island.
Treated the Chasta like they didn't matter. Littered the landing site. Went native.
Killed and ate Chasta.
We needed a Captain Cook to land there. Dumb luck meant that they got a Captain Bligh.
No-one bothered to find out that Chasta Prime was simple and agrarian because they wanted to preserve their homeworld at a rural, park-like level...

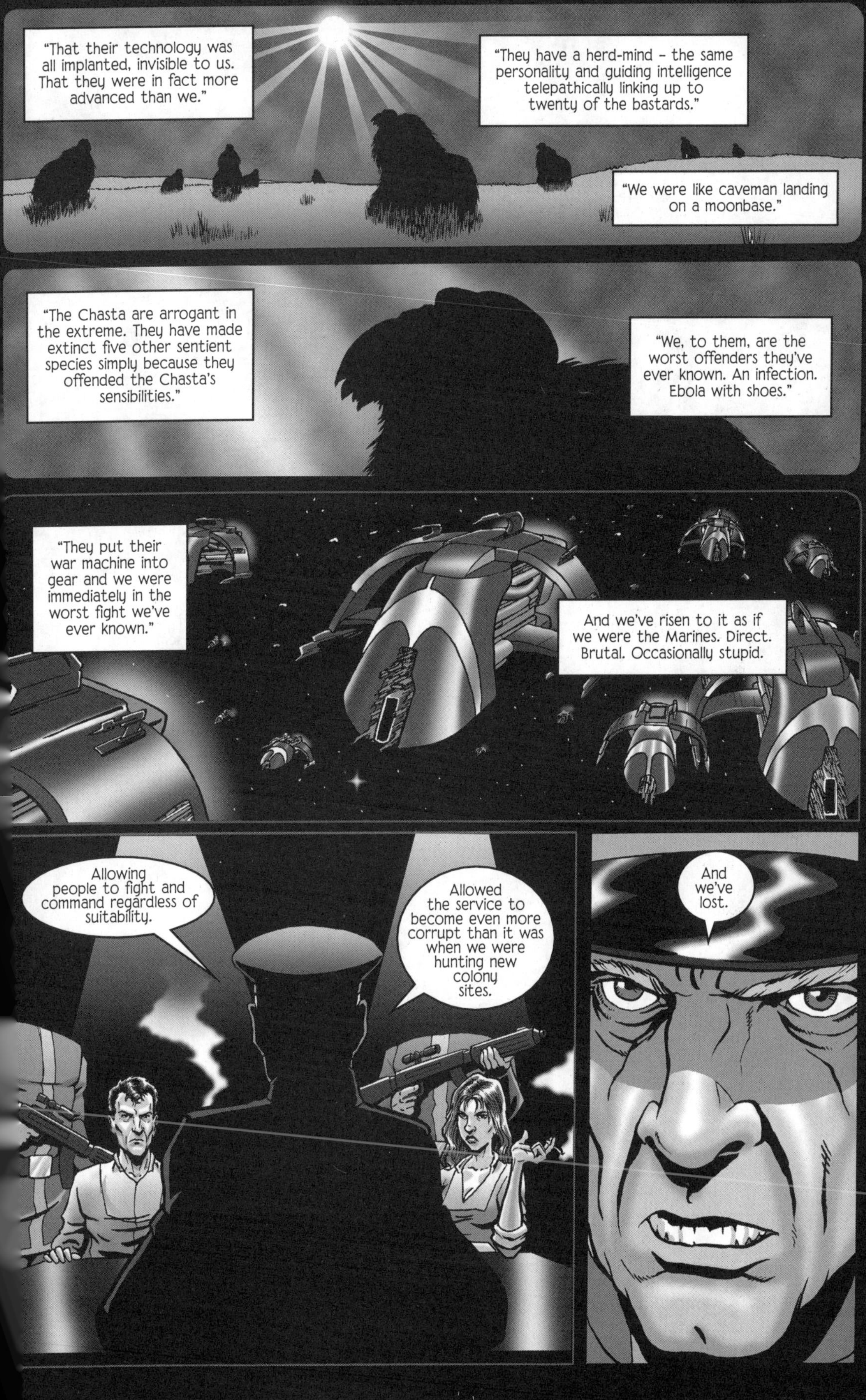
"That their technology was all implanted, invisible to us. That they were in fact more advanced than we."
"They have a herd-mind – the same personality and guiding intelligence telepathically linking up to twenty of the bastards."
"We were like caveman landing on a moonbase."
"The Chasta are arrogant in the extreme. They have made extinct five other sentient species simply because they offended the Chasta's sensibilities."
"We, to them, are the worst offenders they've ever known. An infection. Ebola with shoes."
"They put their war machine into gear and we were immediately in the worst fight we've ever known."
And we've risen to it as if we were the Marines. Direct. Brutal. Occasionally stupid.
Allowing people to fight and command regardless of suitability.
Allowed the service to become even more corrupt than it was when we were hunting new colony sites.
And we've lost.

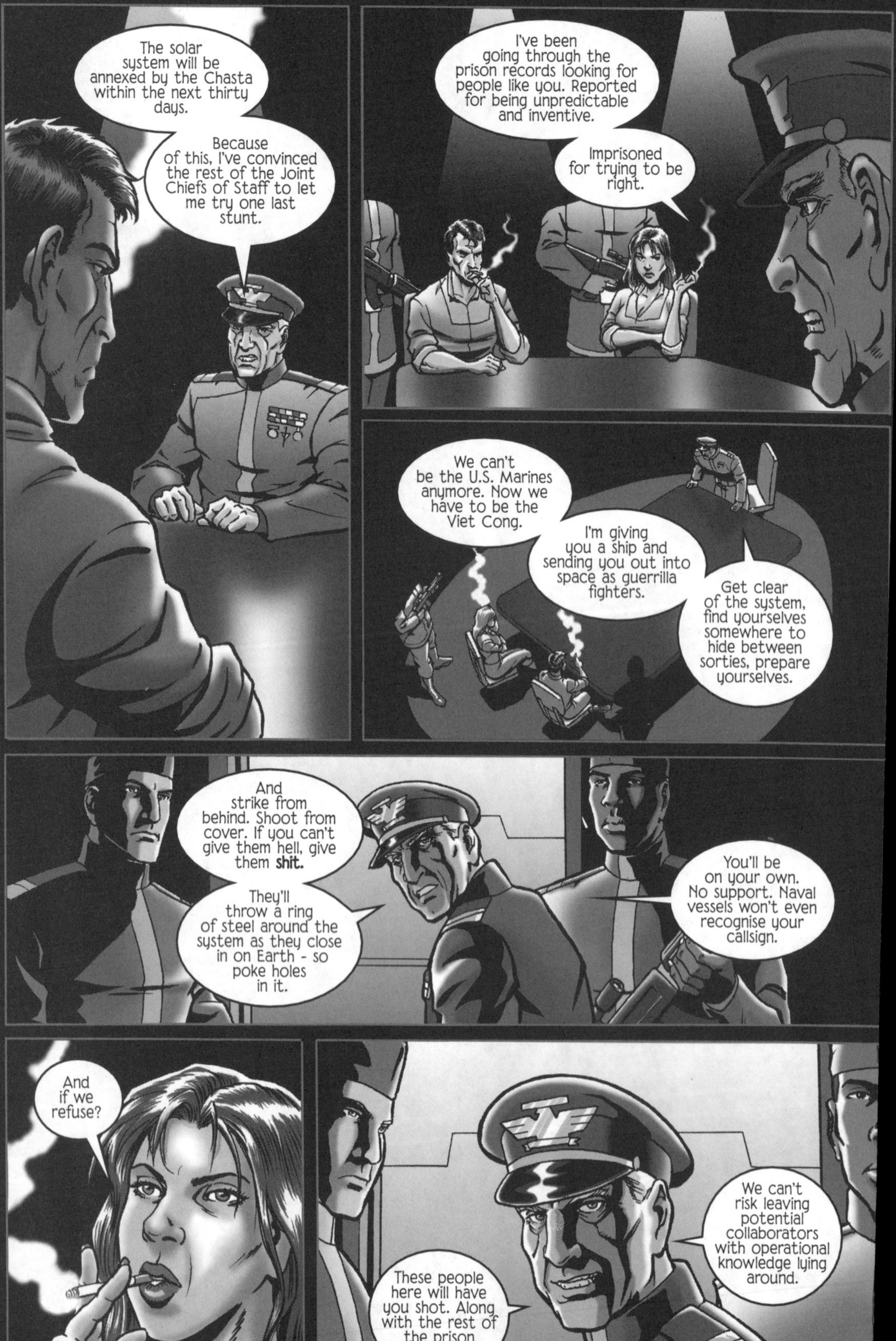
The solar system will be annexed by the Chasta within the next thirty days.
Because of this, I've convinced the rest of the Joint Chiefs of Staff to let me try one last stunt.
I've been going through the prison records looking for people like you. Reported for being unpredictable and inventive.
Imprisoned for trying to be right.
We can't be the U.S. Marines anymore. Now we have to be the Viet Cong.
I'm giving you a ship and sending you out into space as guerrilla fighters.
Get clear of the system, find yourselves somewhere to hide between sorties, prepare yourselves.
And strike from behind. Shoot from cover. If you can't give them hell, give them **shit.**
They'll throw a ring of steel around the system as they close in on Earth - so poke holes in it.
You'll be on your own. No support. Naval vessels won't even recognise your callsign.
And if we refuse?
These people here will have you shot. Along with the rest of the prison populace.
We can't risk leaving potential collaborators with operational knowledge lying around.

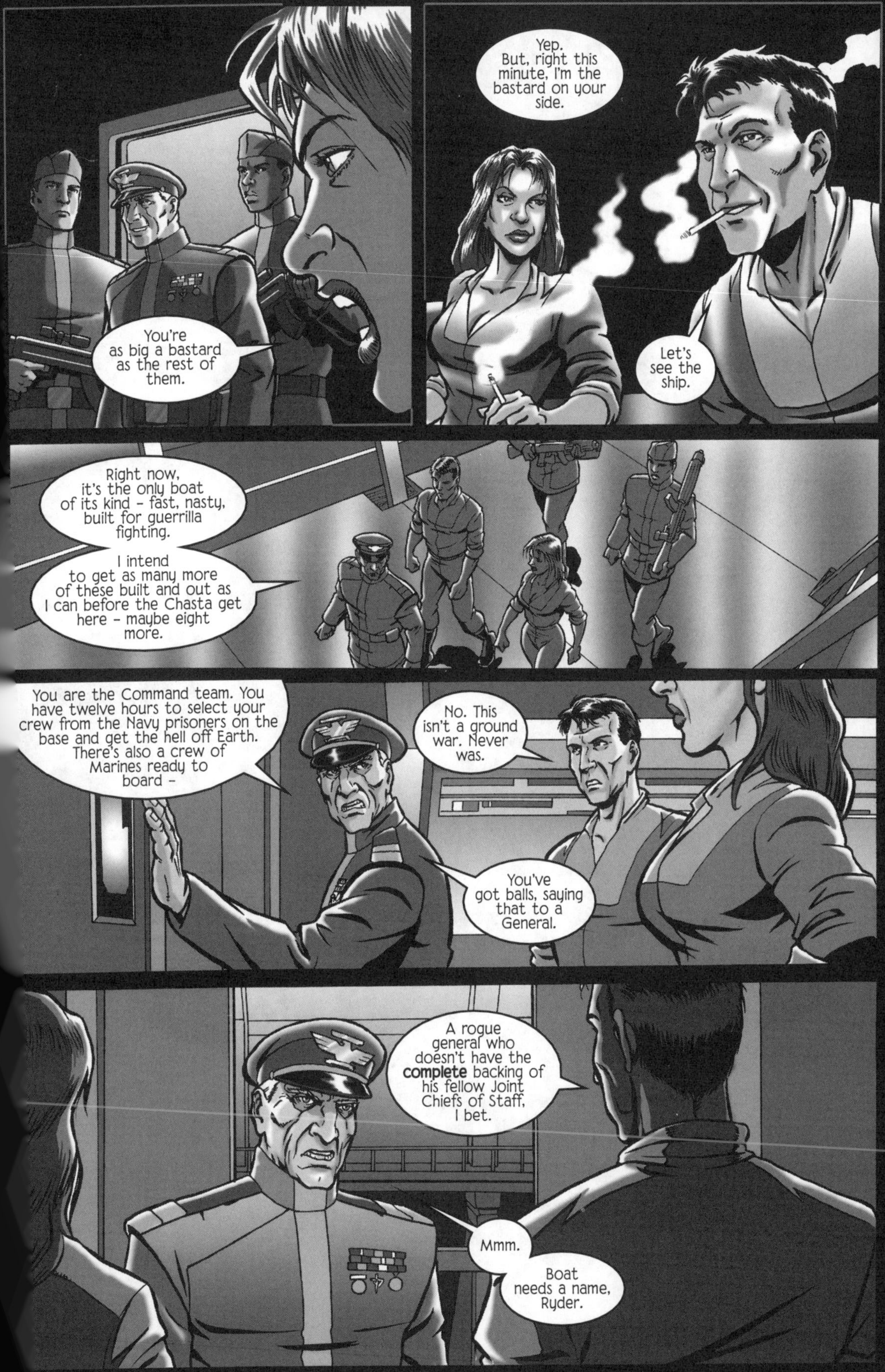
You're as big a bastard as the rest of them.
Yep. But, right this minute, I'm the bastard on your side.
Let's see the ship.
Right now, it's the only boat of its kind - fast, nasty, built for guerrilla fighting.
I intend to get as many more of these built and out as I can before the Chasta get here - maybe eight more.
You are the Command team. You have twelve hours to select your crew from the Navy prisoners on the base and get the hell off Earth. There's also a crew of Marines ready to board -
No. This isn't a ground war. Never was.
You've got balls, saying that to a General.
A rogue general who doesn't have the **complete** backing of his fellow Joint Chiefs of Staff, I bet.
Mmm.
Boat needs a name, Ryder.

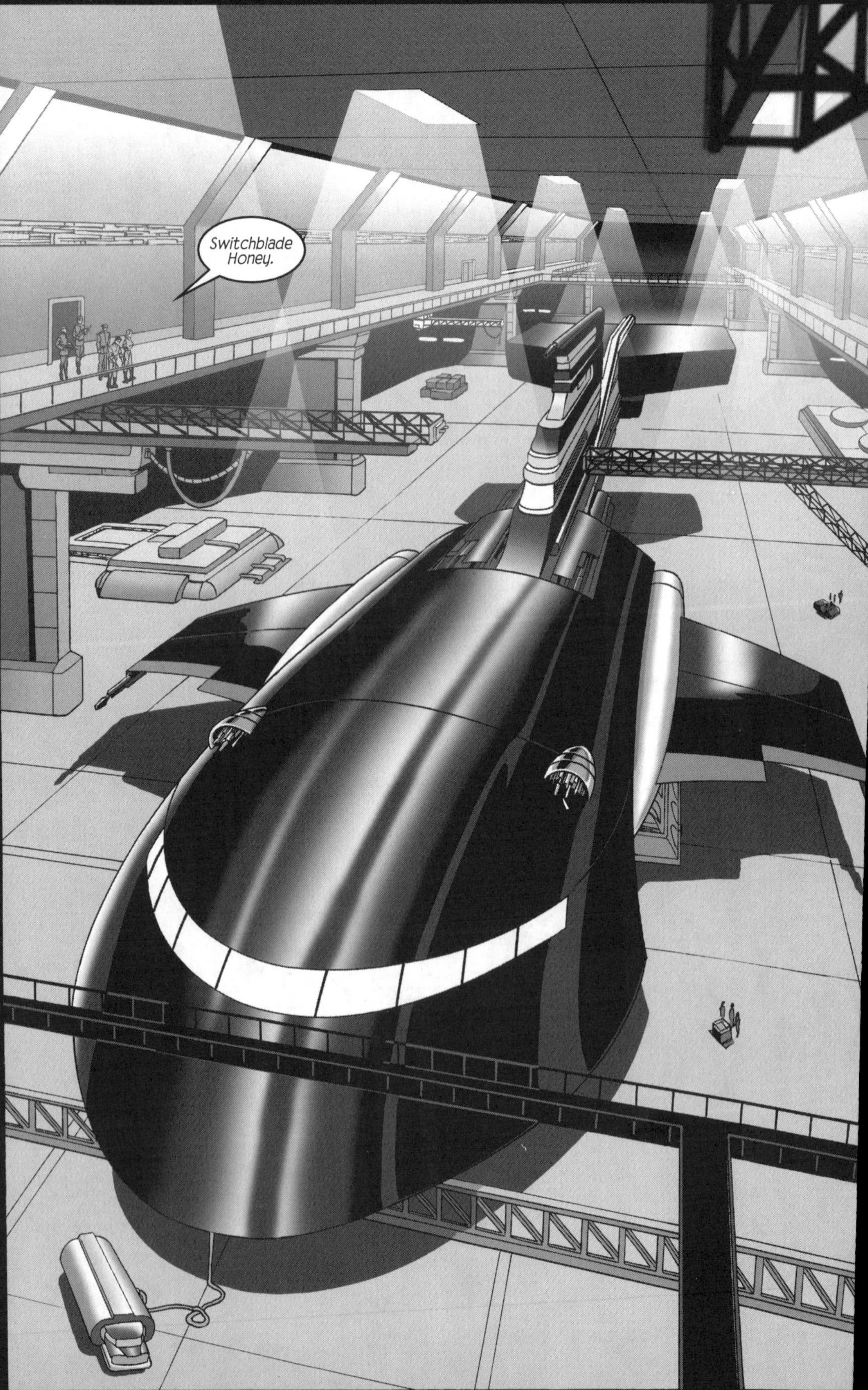
Switchblade Honey.

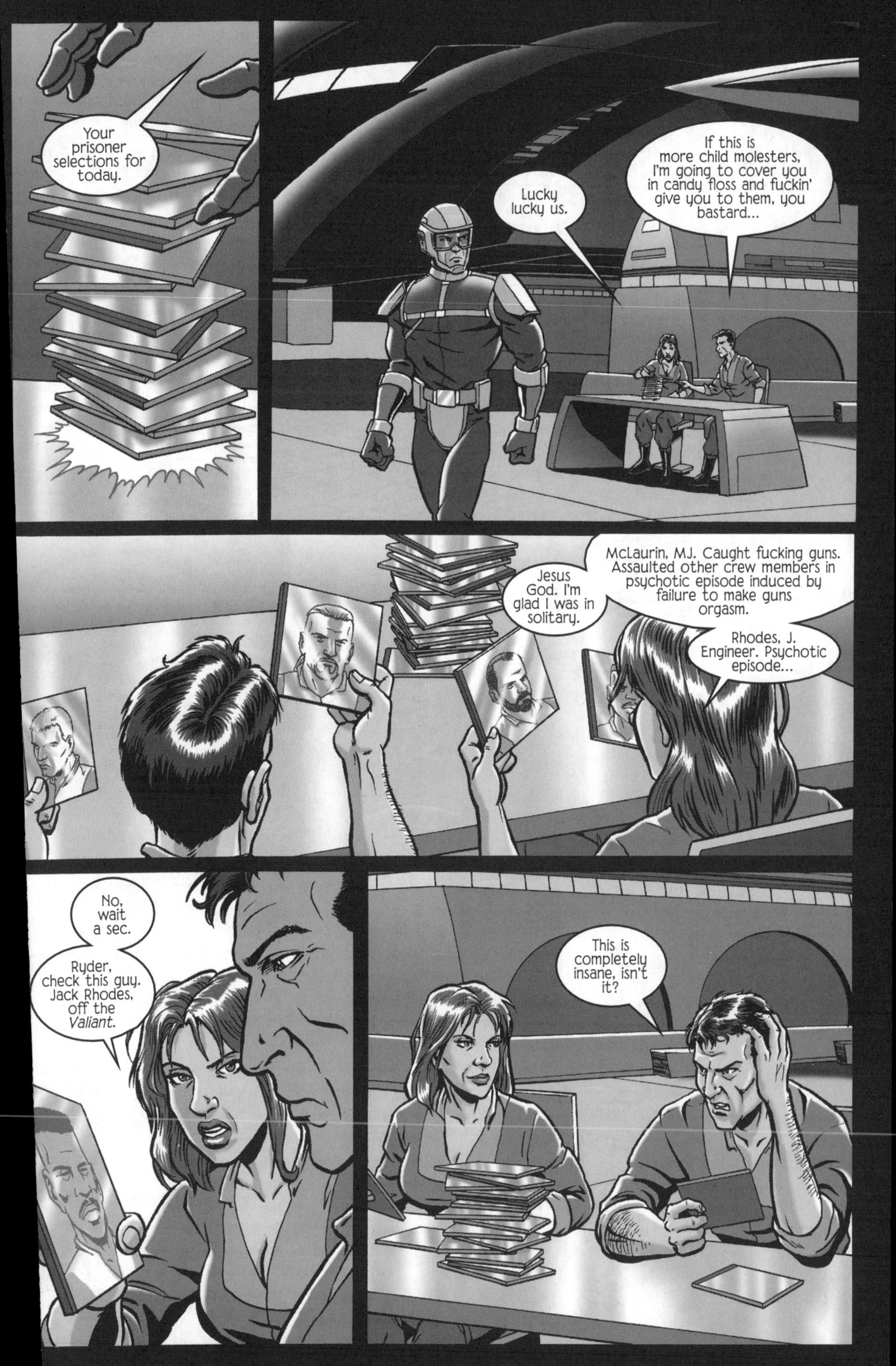
Your prisoner selections for today.
Lucky lucky us.
If this is more child molesters, I'm going to cover you in candy floss and fuckin' give you to them, you bastard...
McLaurin, MJ. Caught fucking guns. Assaulted other crew members in psychotic episode induced by failure to make guns orgasm.
Jesus God. I'm glad I was in solitary.
Rhodes, J. Engineer. Psychotic episode...
No, wait a sec.
Ryder, check this guy. Jack Rhodes, off the *Valiant*.
This is completely insane, isn't it?

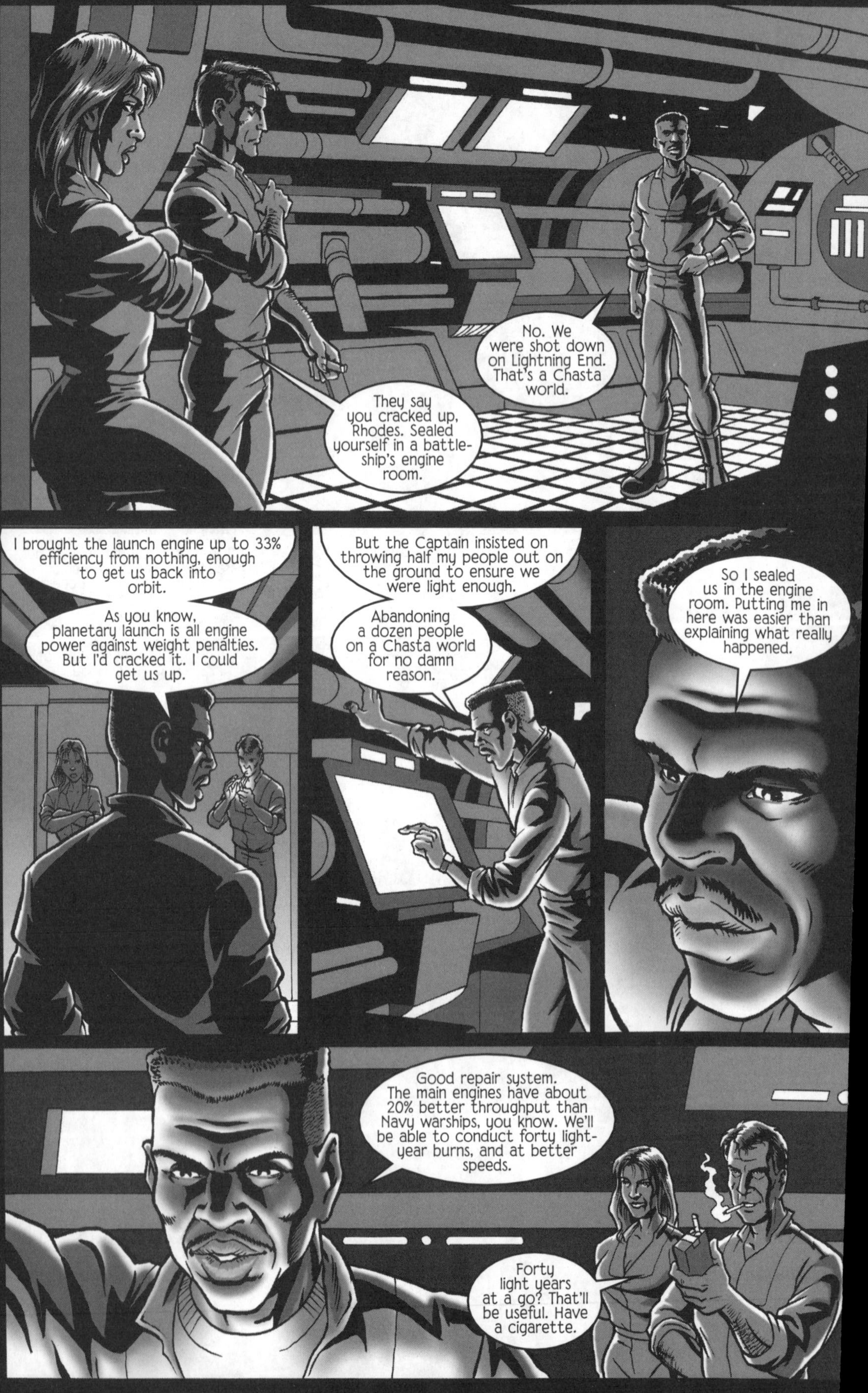
They say you cracked up, Rhodes. Sealed yourself in a battleship's engine room.
No. We were shot down on Lightning End. That's a Chasta world.
I brought the launch engine up to 33% efficiency from nothing, enough to get us back into orbit.
As you know, planetary launch is all engine power against weight penalties. But I'd cracked it. I could get us up.
But the Captain insisted on throwing half my people out on the ground to ensure we were light enough.
Abandoning a dozen people on a Chasta world for no damn reason.
So I sealed us in the engine room. Putting me in here was easier than explaining what really happened.
Good repair system. The main engines have about 20% better throughput than Navy warships, you know. We'll be able to conduct forty light-year burns, and at better speeds.
Forty light years at a go? That'll be useful. Have a cigarette.

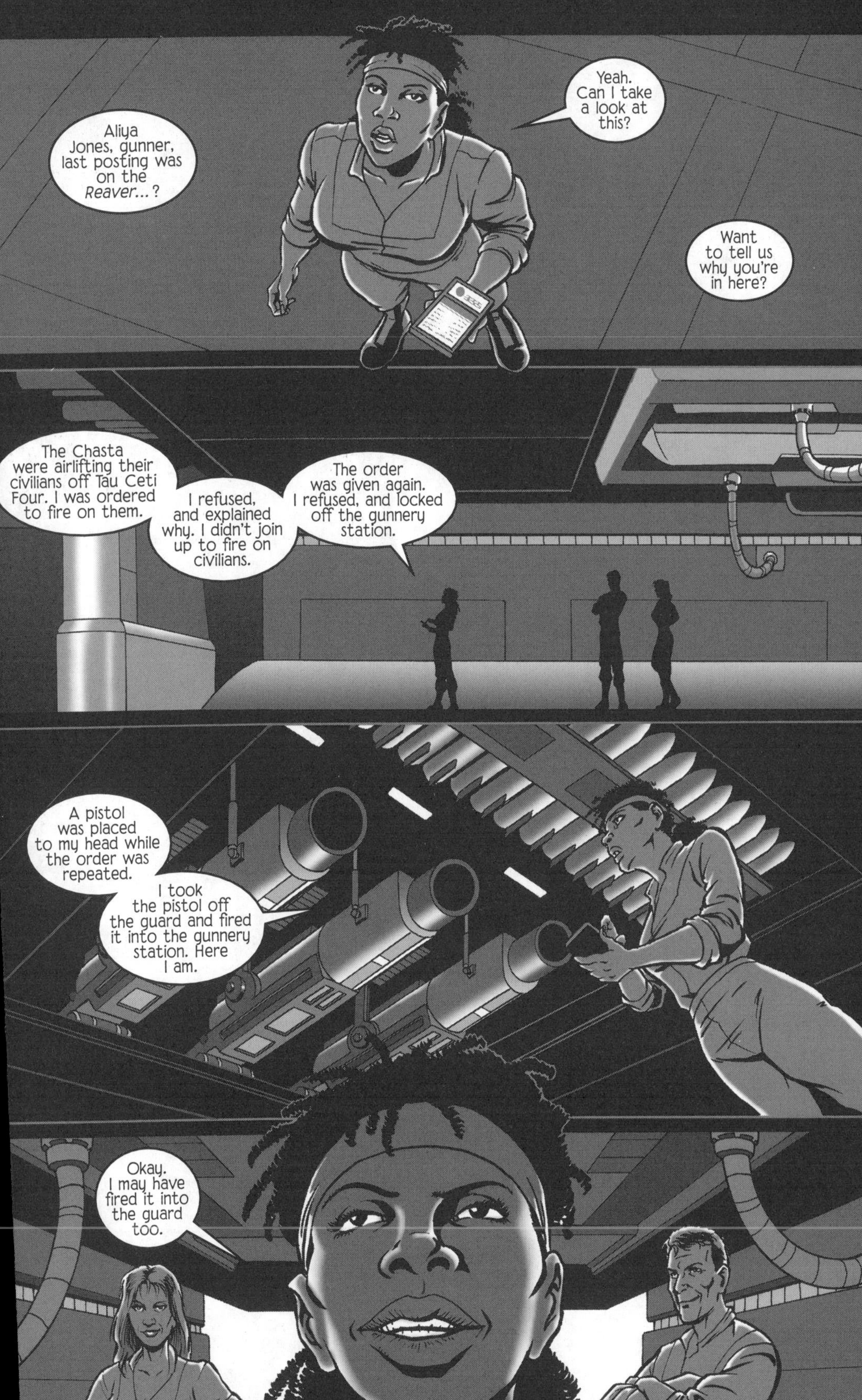
Aliya Jones, gunner, last posting was on the *Reaver*...?
Yeah. Can I take a look at this?
Want to tell us why you're in here?
The Chasta were airlifting their civilians off Tau Ceti Four. I was ordered to fire on them.
I refused, and explained why. I didn't join up to fire on civilians.
The order was given again. I refused, and locked off the gunnery station.
A pistol was placed to my head while the order was repeated.
I took the pistol off the guard and fired it into the gunnery station. Here I am.
Okay. I may have fired it into the guard too.

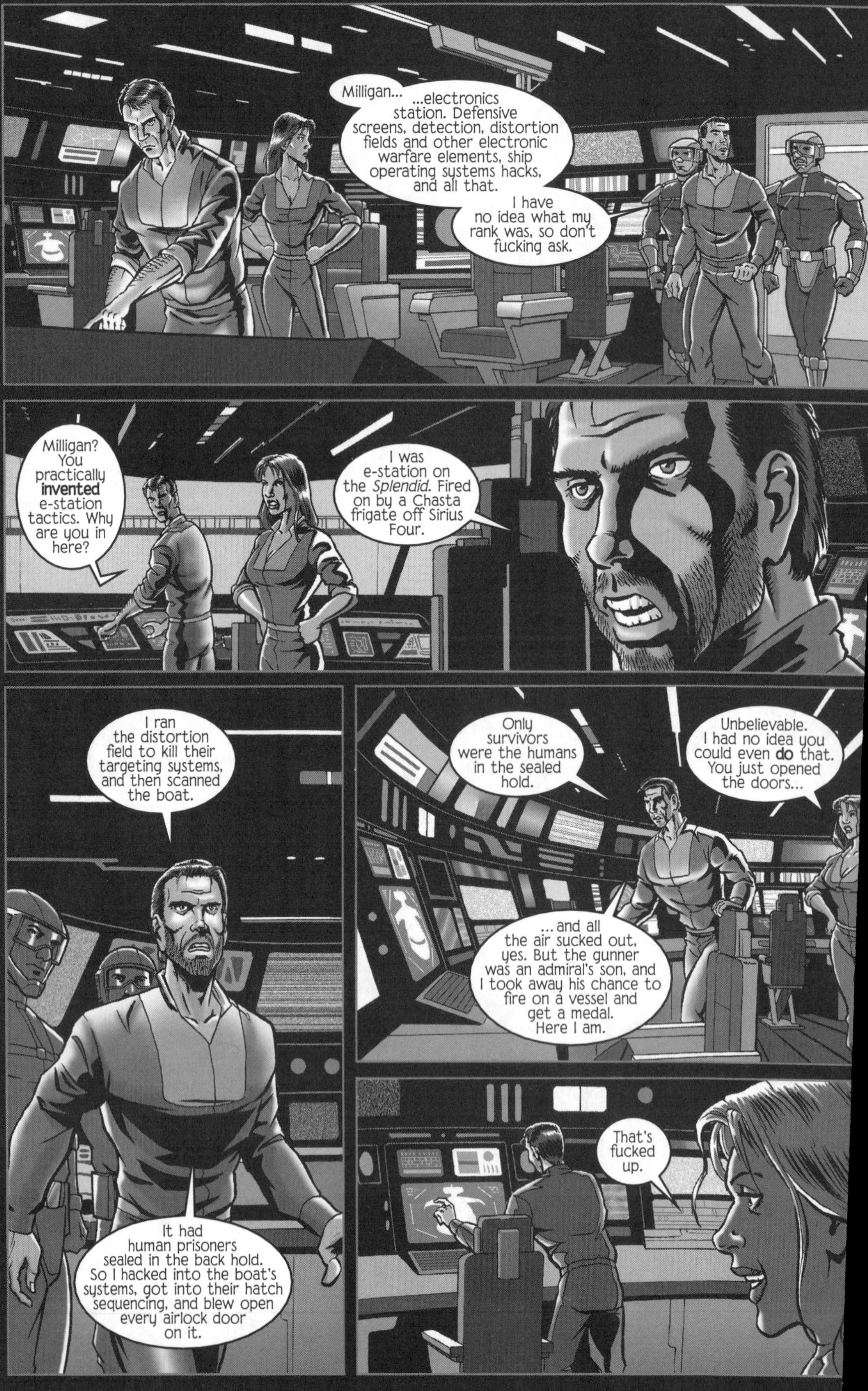

Milligan...
...electronics station. Defensive screens, detection, distortion fields and other electronic warfare elements, ship operating systems hacks, and all that.
I have no idea what my rank was, so don't fucking ask.
Milligan? You practically **invented** e-station tactics. Why are you in here?
I was e-station on the *Splendid*. Fired on by a Chasta frigate off Sirius Four.
I ran the distortion field to kill their targeting systems, and then scanned the boat.
It had human prisoners sealed in the back hold. So I hacked into the boat's systems, got into their hatch sequencing, and blew open every airlock door on it.
Only survivors were the humans in the sealed hold.
Unbelievable. I had no idea you could even **do** that. You just opened the doors...
...and all the air sucked out, yes. But the gunner was an admiral's son, and I took away his chance to fire on a vessel and get a medal. Here I am.
That's fucked up.

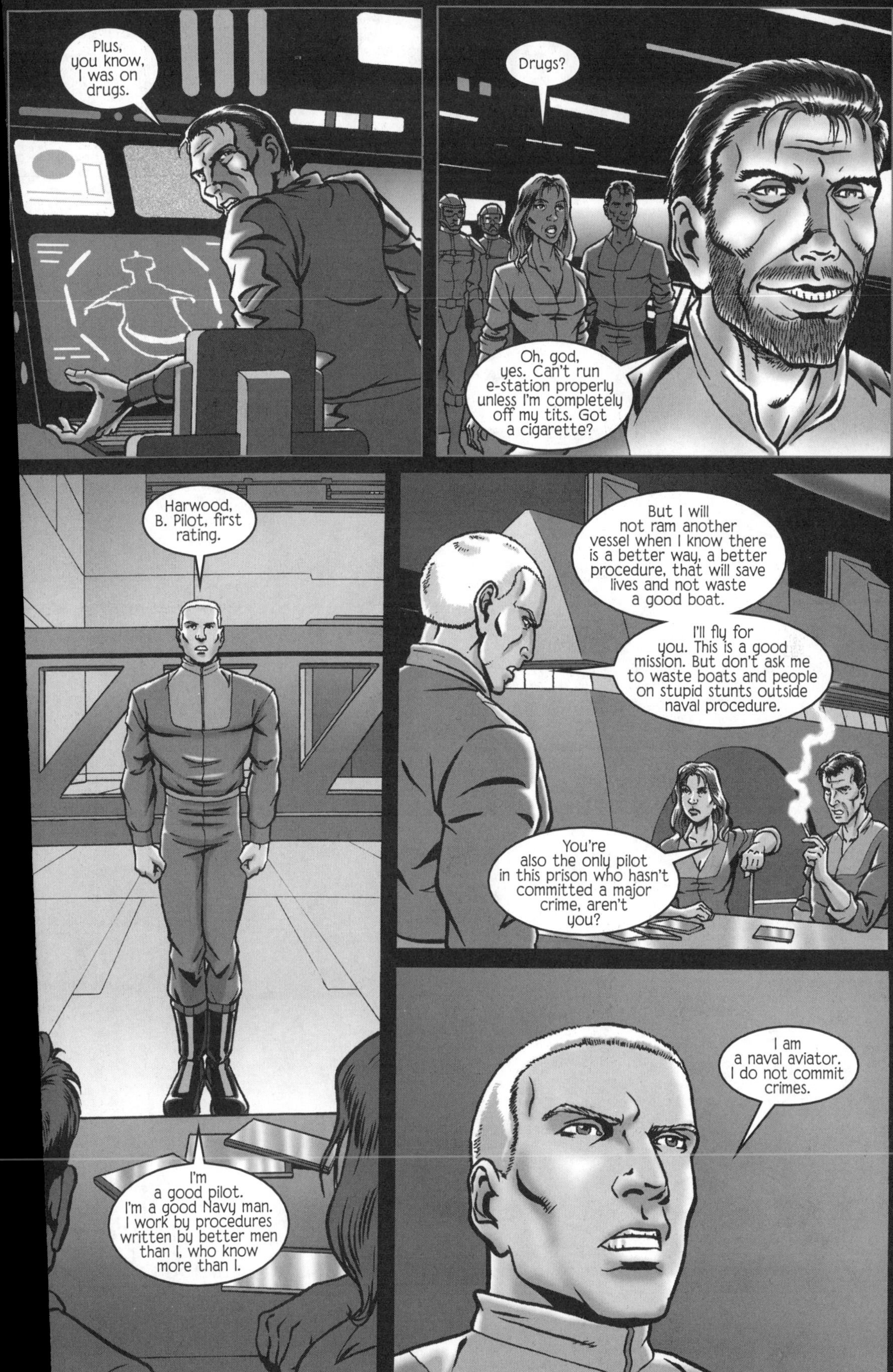
Plus, you know, I was on drugs.
Drugs?
Oh, god, yes. Can't run e-station properly unless I'm completely off my tits. Got a cigarette?
Harwood, B. Pilot, first rating.
I'm a good pilot. I'm a good Navy man. I work by procedures written by better men than I, who know more than I.
But I will not ram another vessel when I know there is a better way, a better procedure, that will save lives and not waste a good boat.
I'll fly for you. This is a good mission. But don't ask me to waste boats and people on stupid stunts outside naval procedure.
You're also the only pilot in this prison who hasn't committed a major crime, aren't you?
I am a naval aviator. I do not commit crimes.

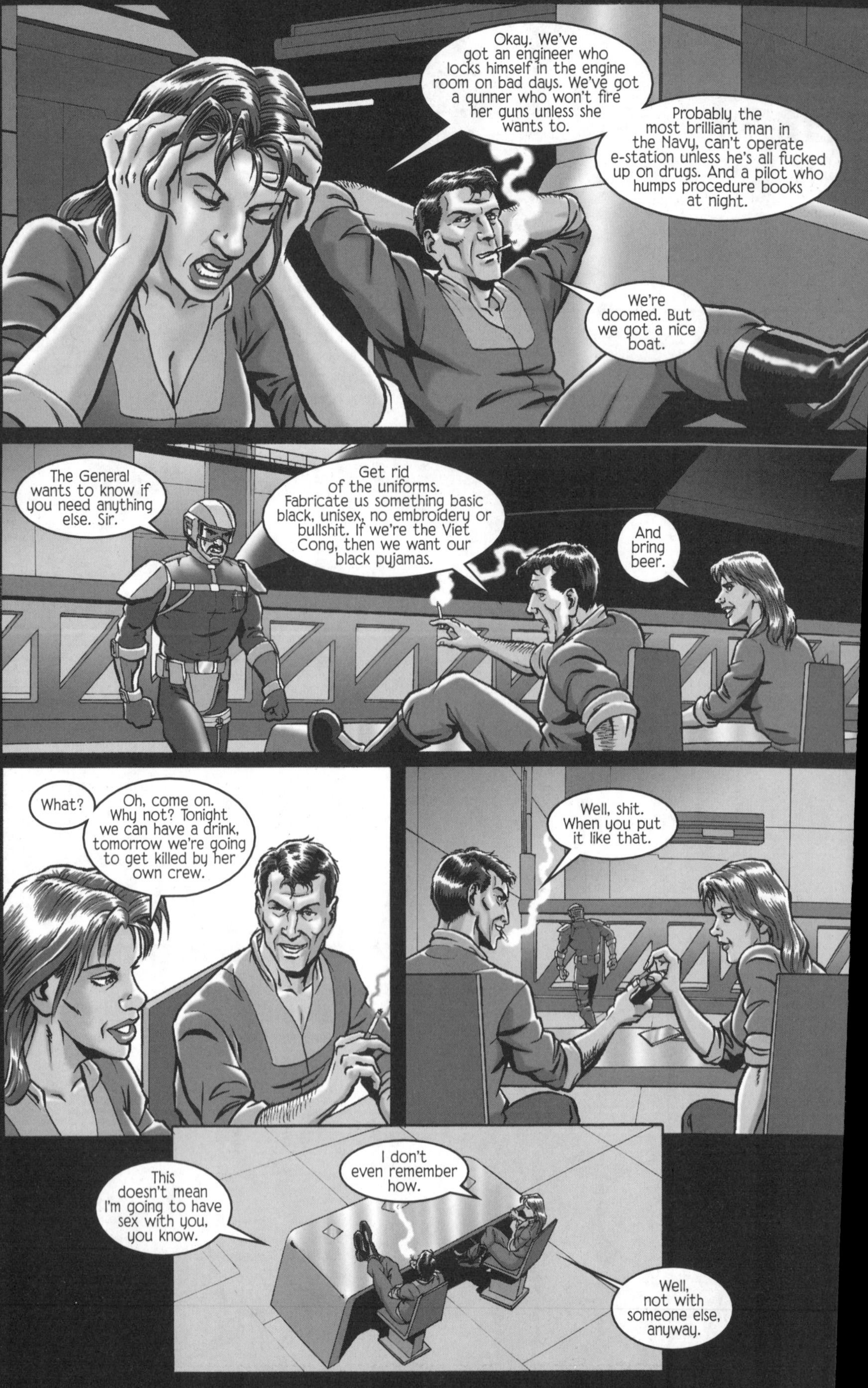

Okay. We've got an engineer who locks himself in the engine room on bad days. We've got a gunner who won't fire her guns unless she wants to.
Probably the most brilliant man in the Navy, can't operate e-station unless he's all fucked up on drugs. And a pilot who humps procedure books at night.
We're doomed. But we got a nice boat.
The General wants to know if you need anything else. Sir.
Get rid of the uniforms. Fabricate us something basic black, unisex, no embroidery or bullshit. If we're the Viet Cong, then we want our black pyjamas.
And bring beer.
What?
Oh, come on. Why not? Tonight we can have a drink, tomorrow we're going to get killed by her own crew.
Well, shit. When you put it like that.
This doesn't mean I'm going to have sex with you, you know.
I don't even remember how.
Well, not with someone else, anyway.

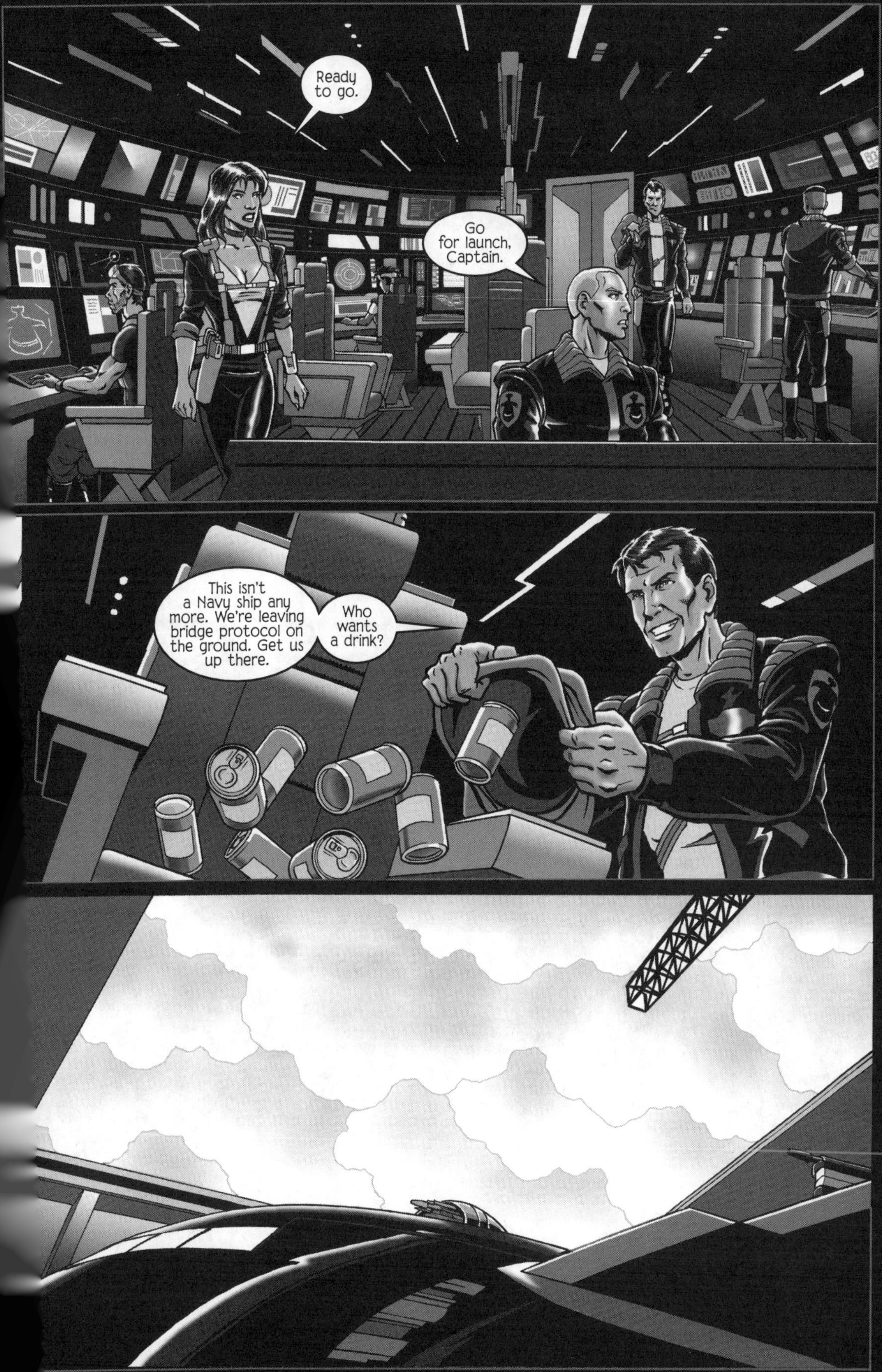
Ready to go.
Go for launch, Captain.
This isn't a Navy ship any more. We're leaving bridge protocol on the ground. Get us up there.
Who wants a drink?

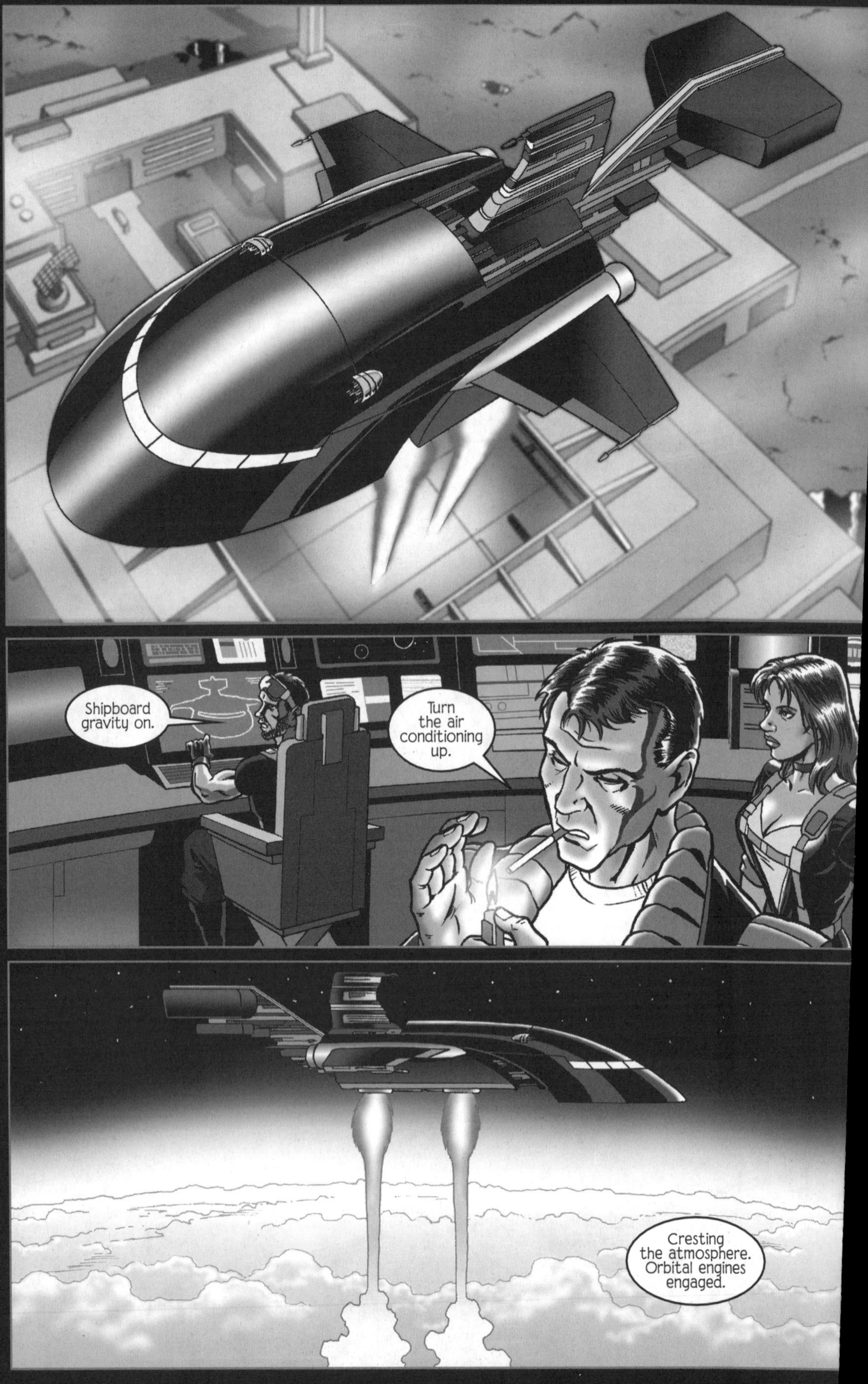
Shipboard gravity on.
Turn the air conditioning up.
Cresting the atmosphere. Orbital engines engaged.

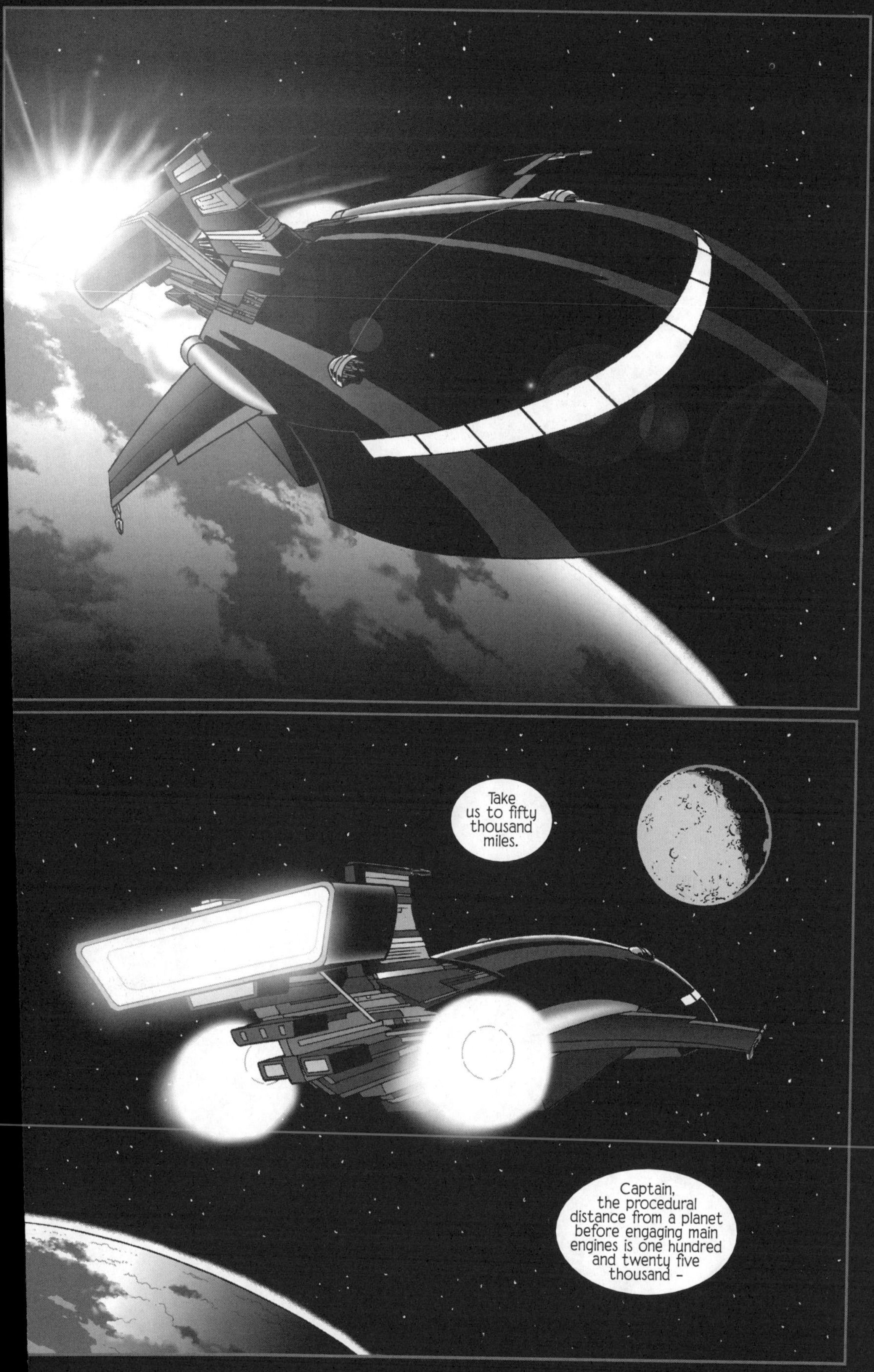
Take us to fifty thousand miles.
Captain, the procedural distance from a planet before engaging main engines is one hundred and twenty five thousand -

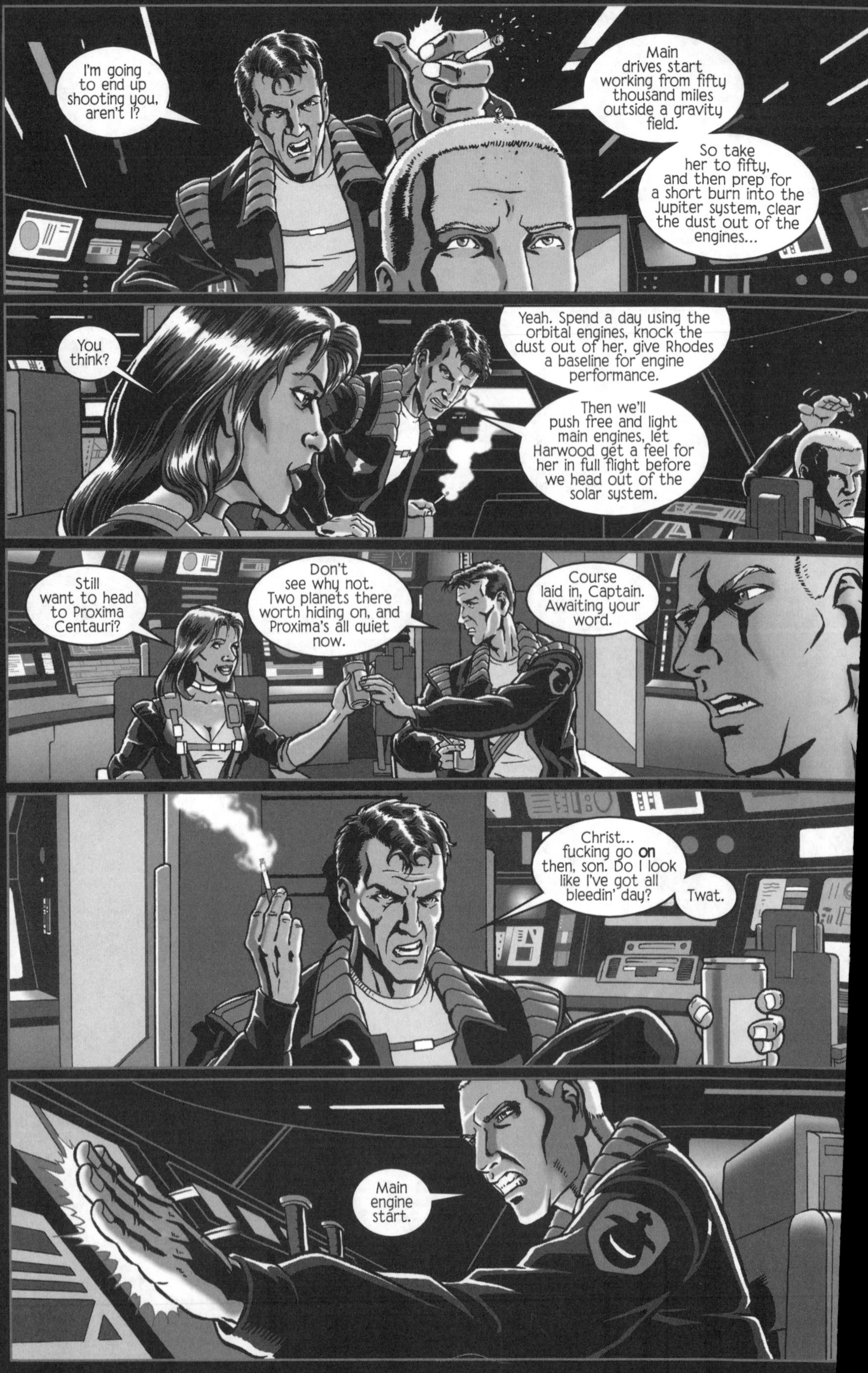
I'm going to end up shooting you, aren't I?
Main drives start working from fifty thousand miles outside a gravity field.
So take her to fifty, and then prep for a short burn into the Jupiter system, clear the dust out of the engines...
You think?
Yeah. Spend a day using the orbital engines, knock the dust out of her, give Rhodes a baseline for engine performance.
Then we'll push free and light main engines, let Harwood get a feel for her in full flight before we head out of the solar system.
Still want to head to Proxima Centauri?
Don't see why not. Two planets there worth hiding on, and Proxima's all quiet now.
Course laid in, Captain. Awaiting your word.
Christ... fucking go **on** then, son. Do I look like I've got all bleedin' day?
Twat.
Main engine start.

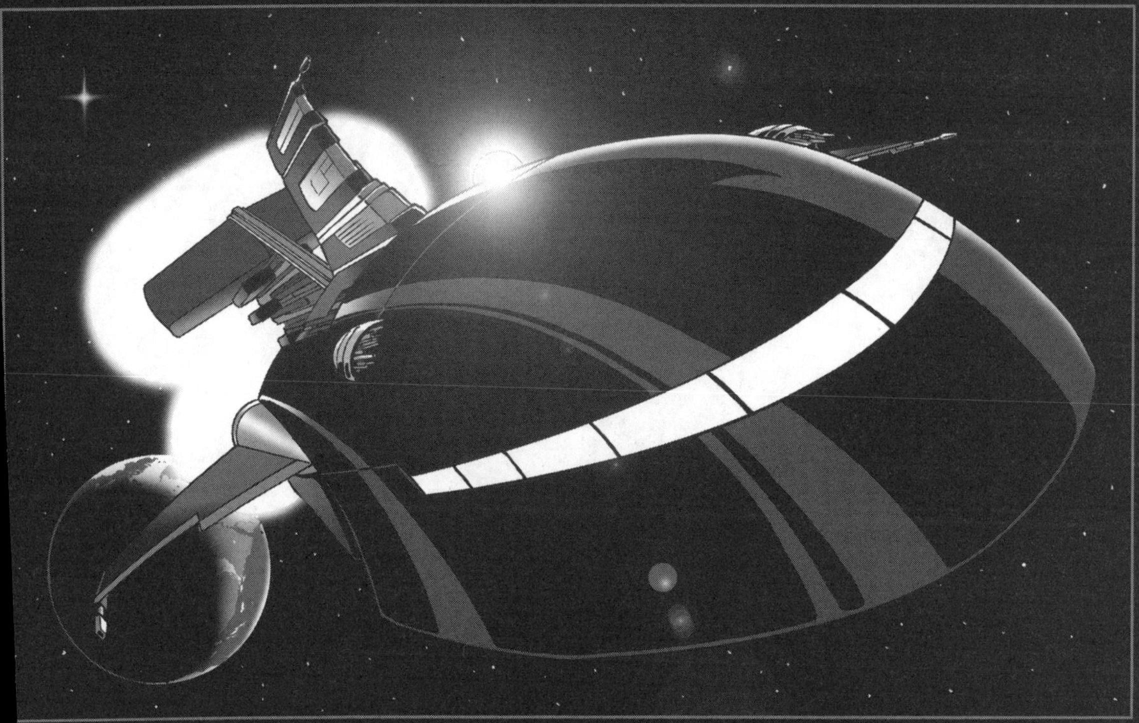

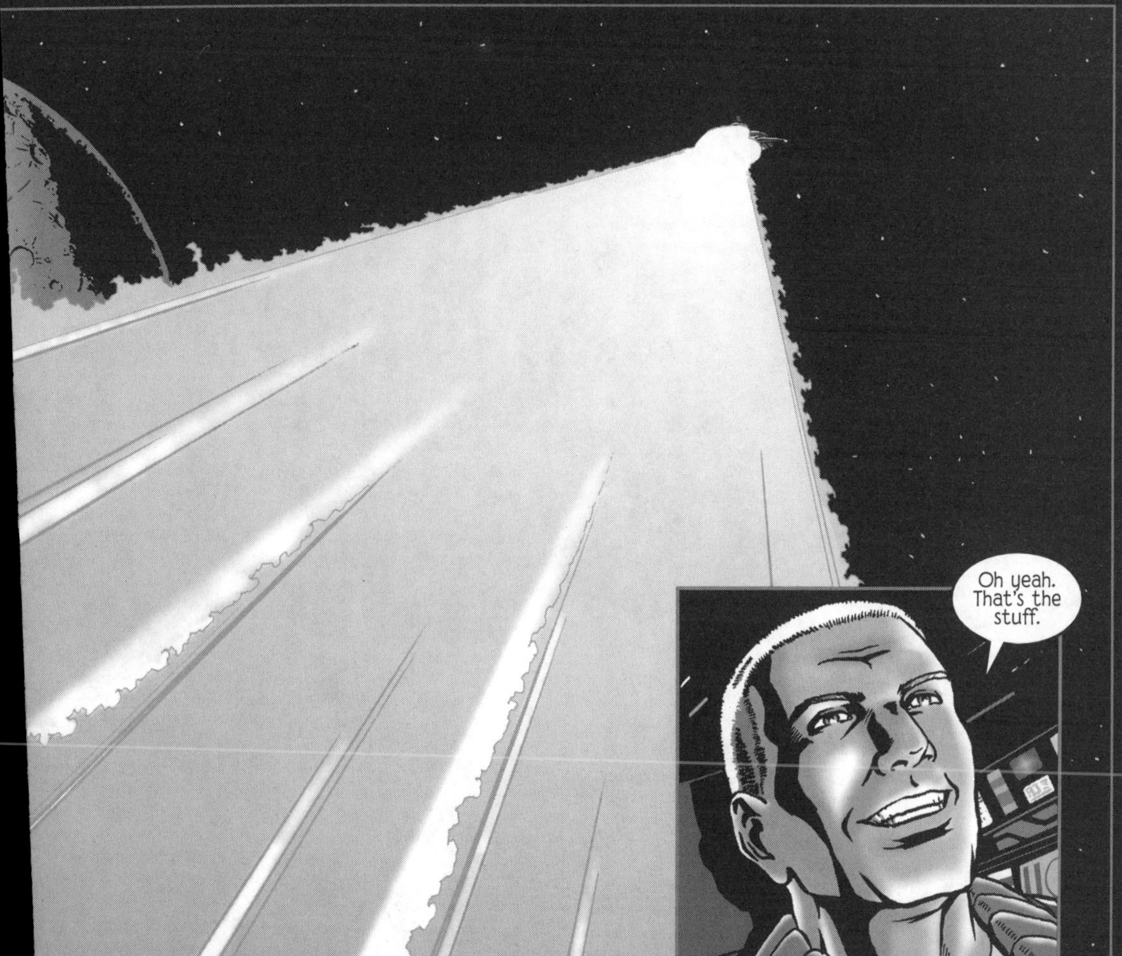
Oh yeah. That's the stuff.

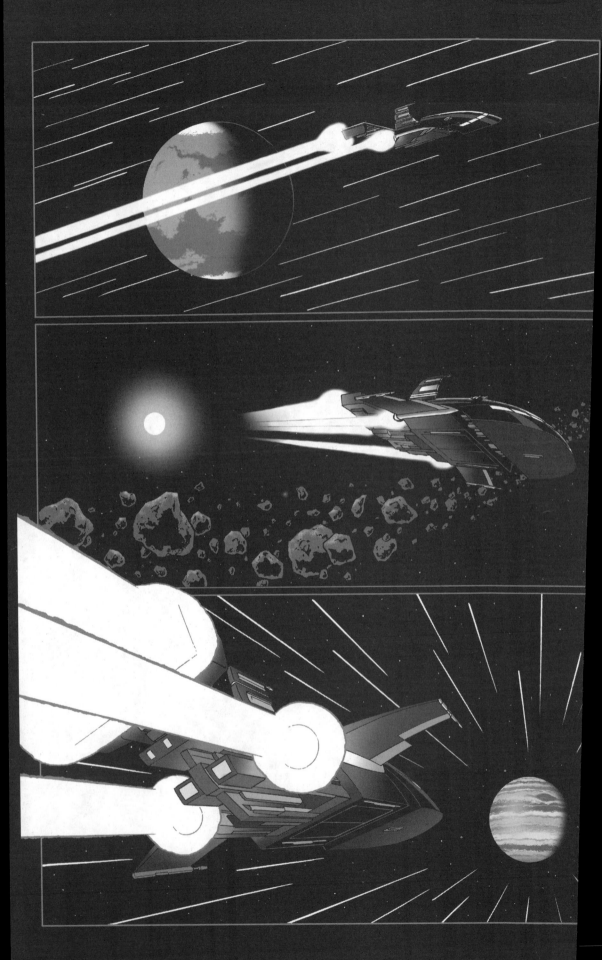

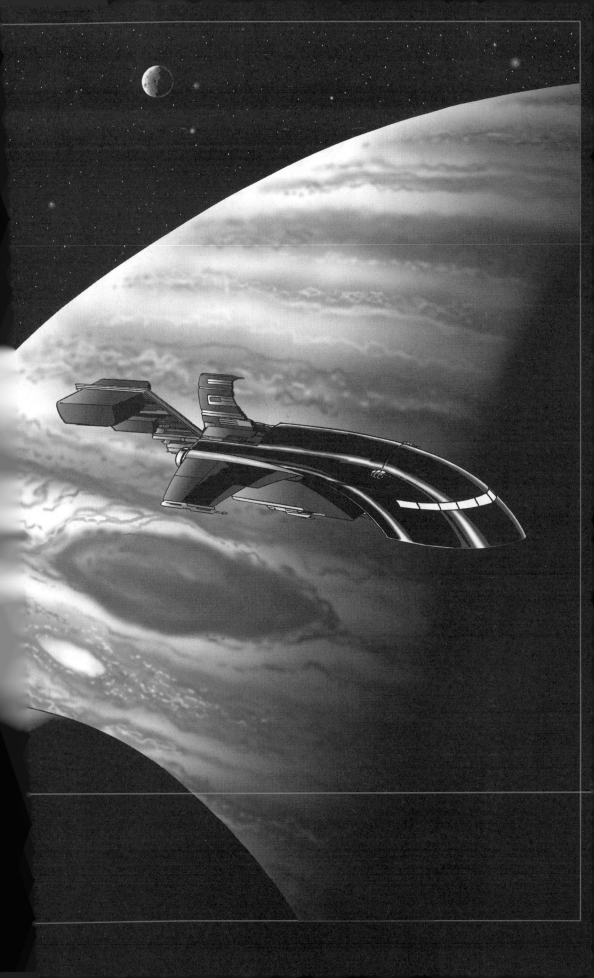

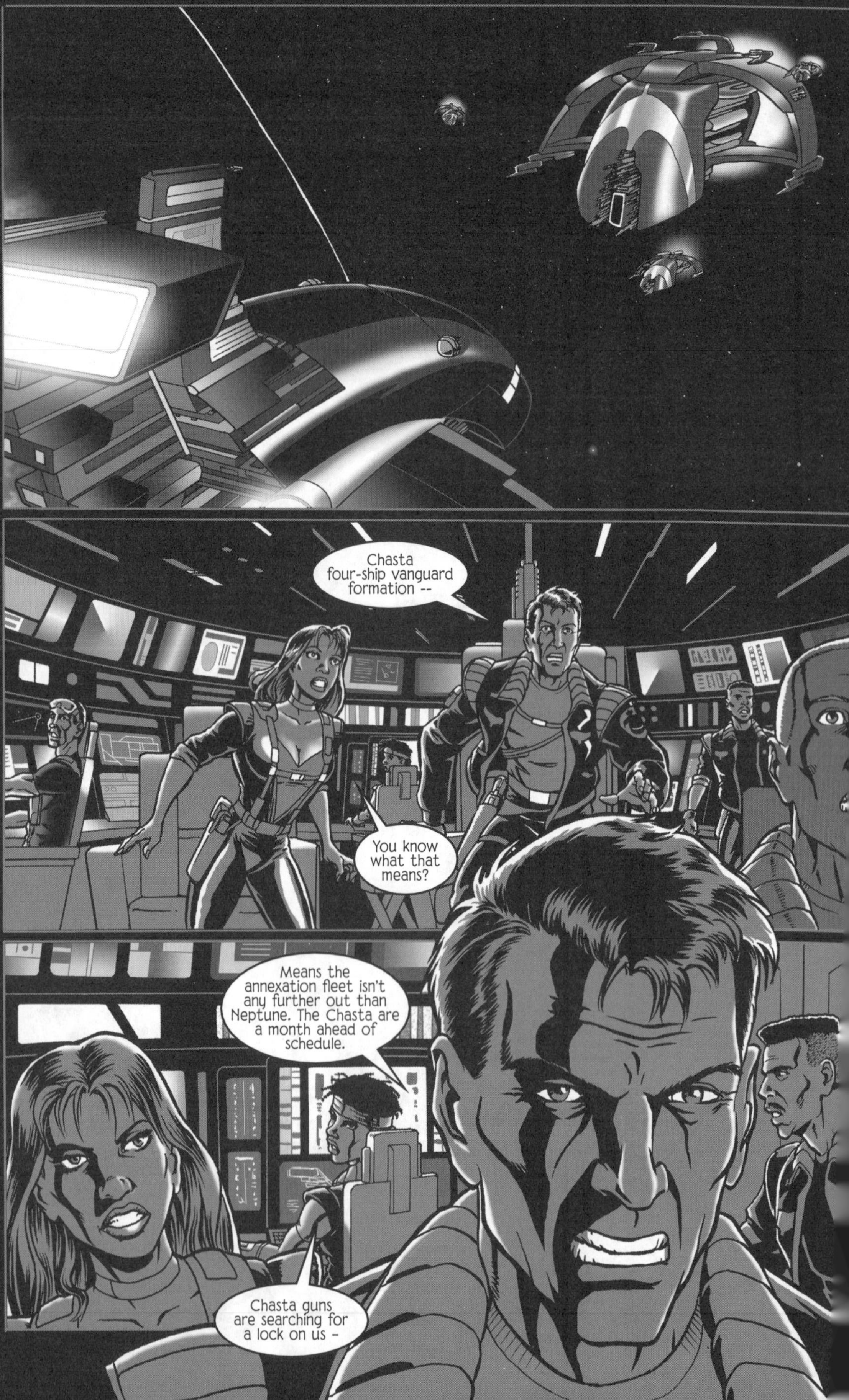

Chasta four-ship vanguard formation --
You know what that means?
Means the annexation fleet isn't any further out than Neptune. The Chasta are a month ahead of schedule.
Chasta guns are searching for a lock on us -

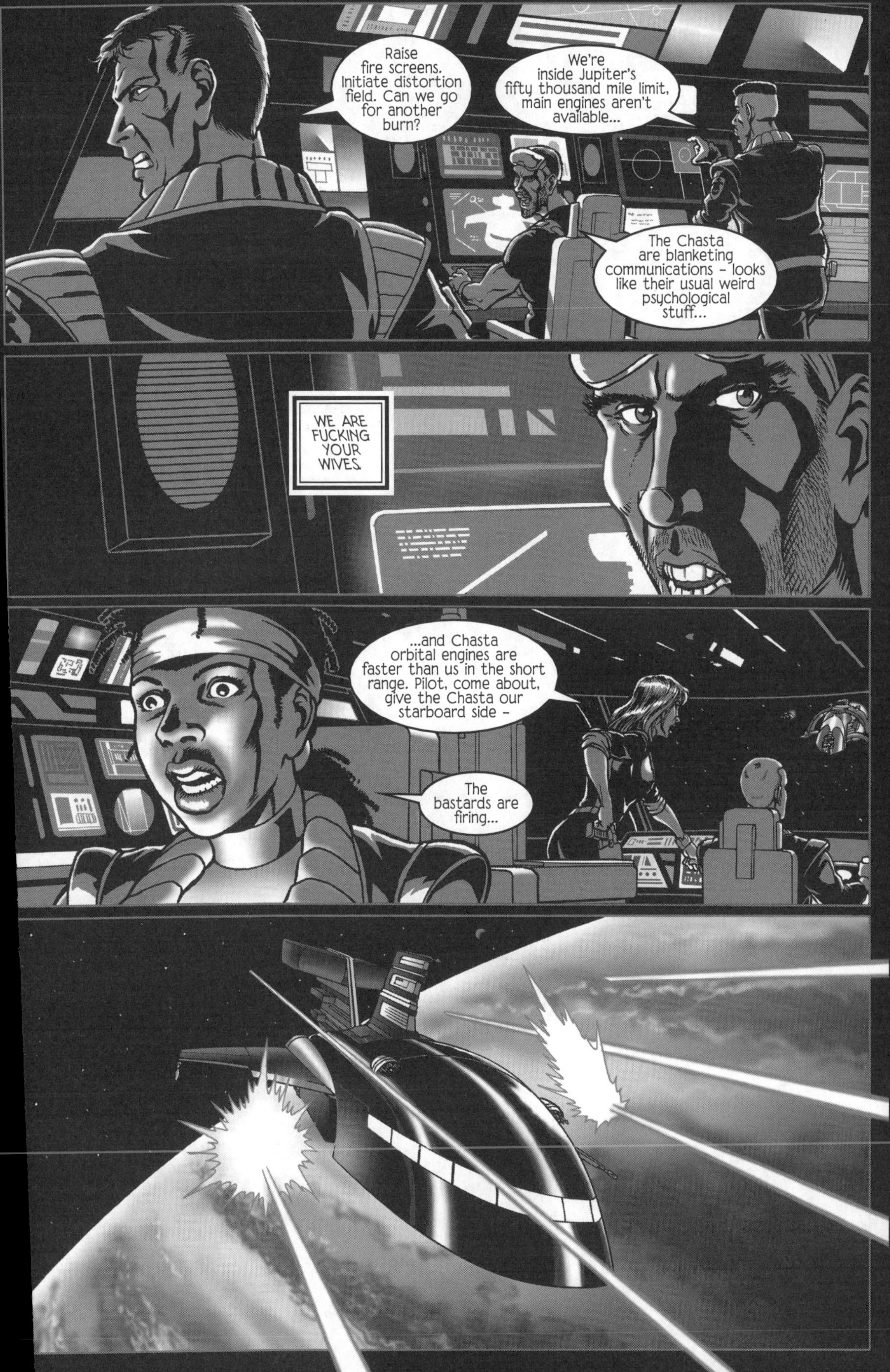
Raise fire screens. Initiate distortion field. Can we go for another burn?
We're inside Jupiter's fifty thousand mile limit, main engines aren't available...
The Chasta are blanketing communications - looks like their usual weird psychological stuff...
WE ARE FUCKING YOUR WIVES
...and Chasta orbital engines are faster than us in the short range. Pilot, come about, give the Chasta our starboard side -
The bastards are firing...

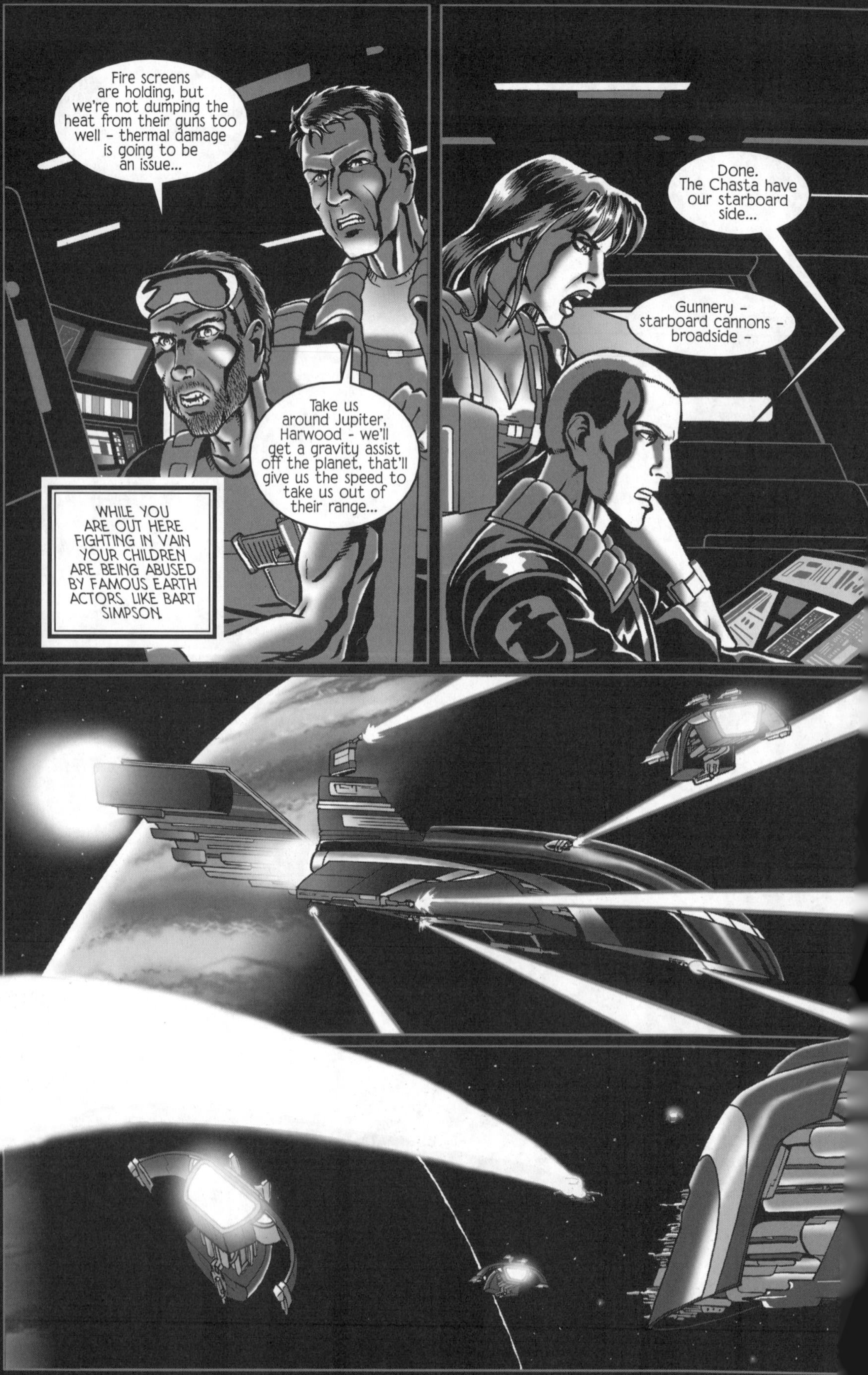

Fire screens are holding, but we're not dumping the heat from their guns too well - thermal damage is going to be an issue...
Take us around Jupiter, Harwood - we'll get a gravity assist off the planet, that'll give us the speed to take us out of their range...
WHILE YOU ARE OUT HERE FIGHTING IN VAIN YOUR CHILDREN ARE BEING ABUSED BY FAMOUS EARTH ACTORS LIKE BART SIMPSON.
Done. The Chasta have our starboard side...
Gunnery - starboard cannons - broadside -

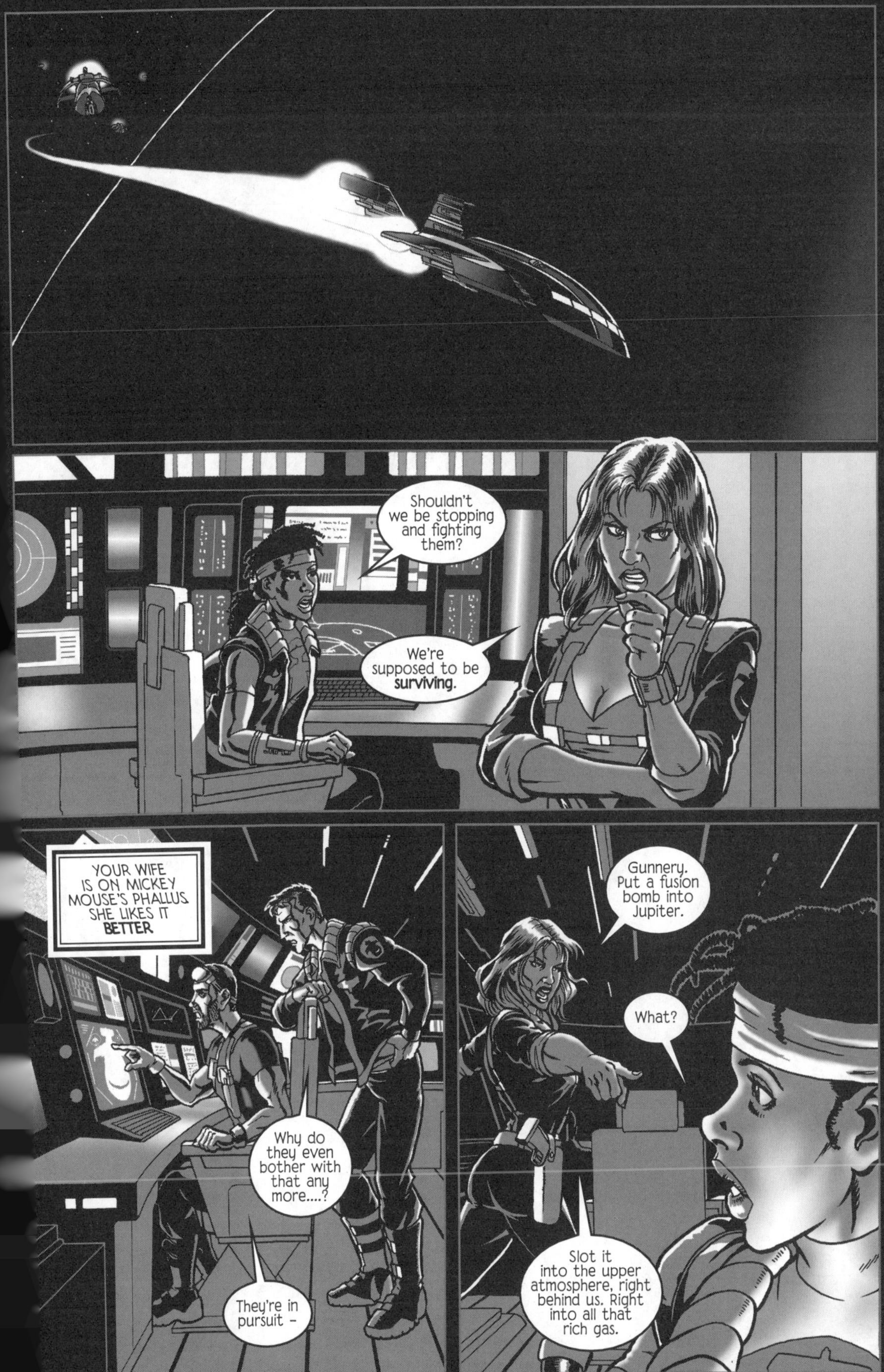

Shouldn't we be stopping and fighting them?
We're supposed to be **surviving**.
YOUR WIFE IS ON MICKEY MOUSE'S PHALLUS. SHE LIKES IT **BETTER**
Why do they even bother with that any more....?
They're in pursuit -
Gunnery. Put a fusion bomb into Jupiter.
What?
Slot it into the upper atmosphere, right behind us. Right into all that rich gas.

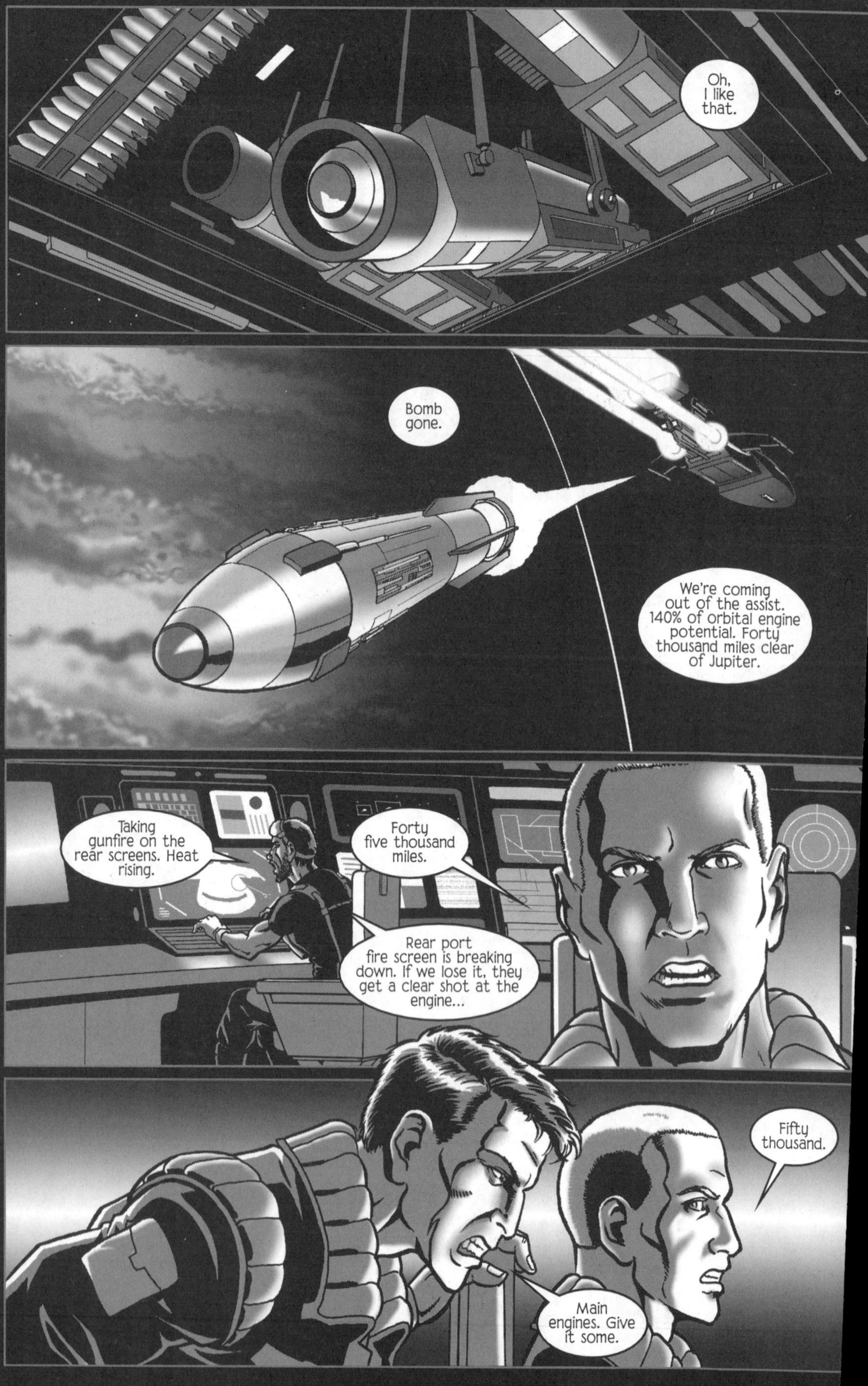
Oh, I like that.
Bomb gone.
We're coming out of the assist. 140% of orbital engine potential. Forty thousand miles clear of Jupiter.
Taking gunfire on the rear screens. Heat rising.
Forty five thousand miles.
Rear port fire screen is breaking down. If we lose it, they get a clear shot at the engine...
Fifty thousand.
Main engines. Give it some.

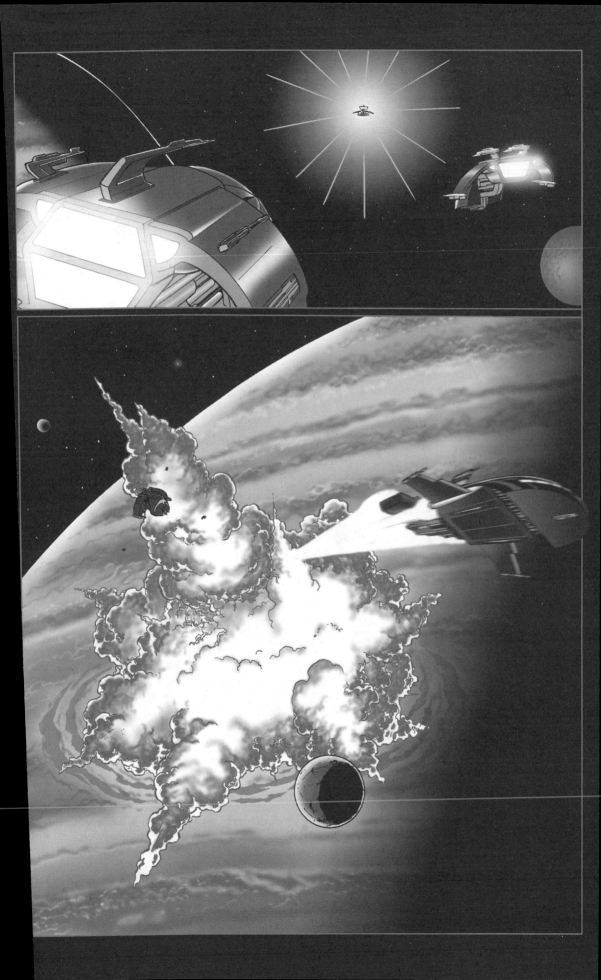

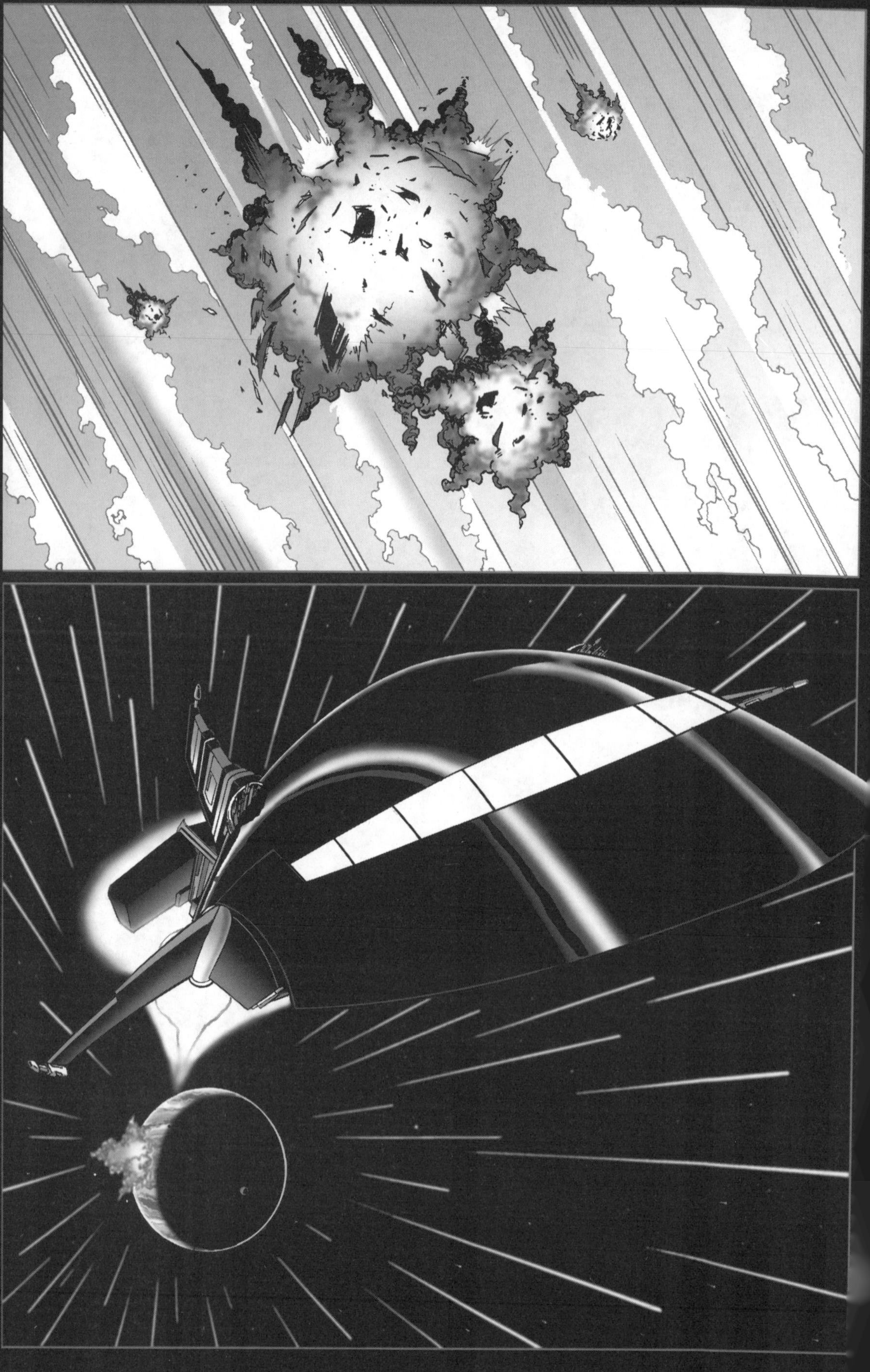

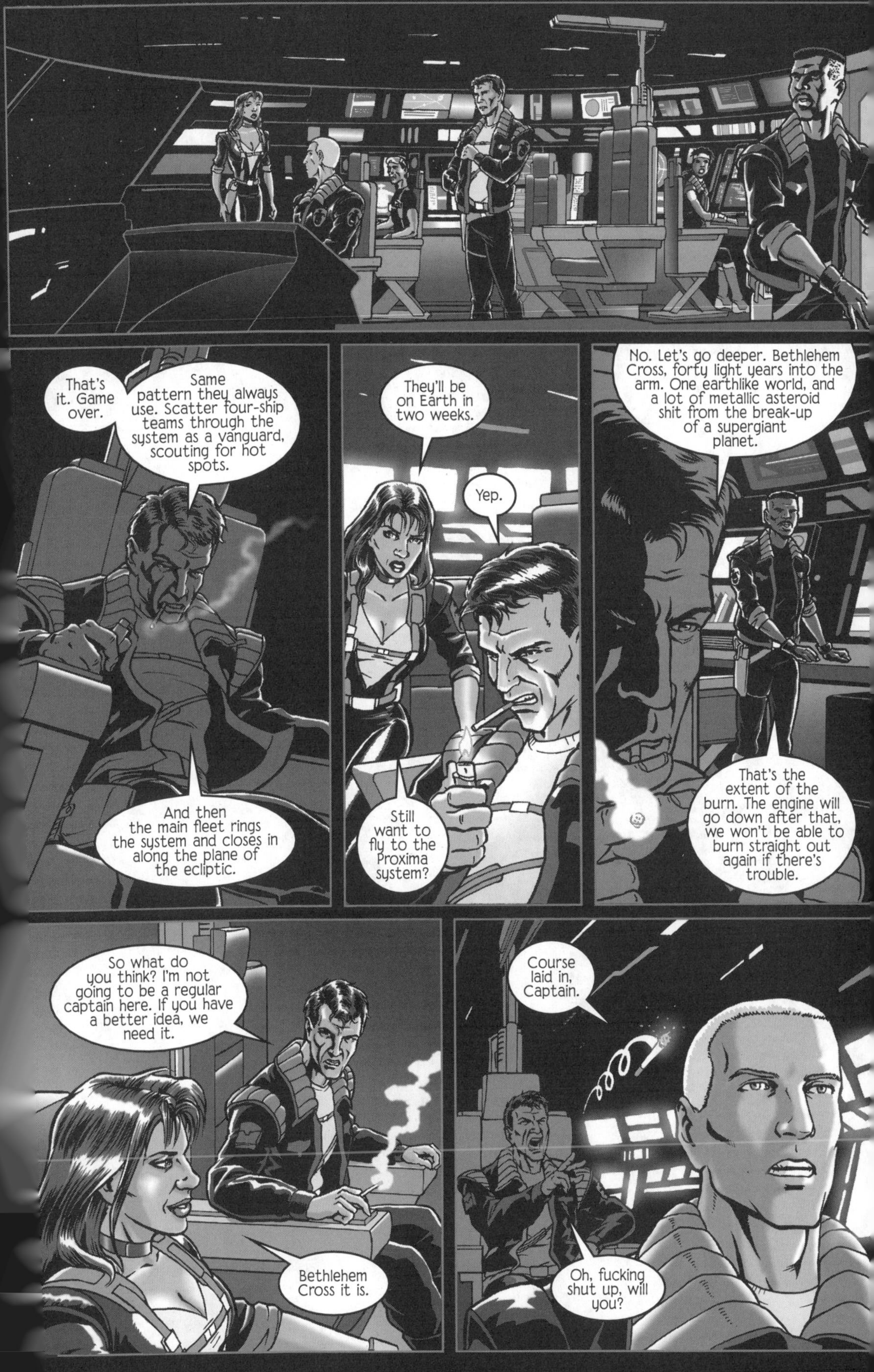
That's it. Game over.
Same pattern they always use. Scatter four-ship teams through the system as a vanguard, scouting for hot spots.
And then the main fleet rings the system and closes in along the plane of the ecliptic.
They'll be on Earth in two weeks.
Yep.
Still want to fly to the Proxima system?
No. Let's go deeper. Bethlehem Cross, forty light years into the arm. One earthlike world, and a lot of metallic asteroid shit from the break-up of a supergiant planet.
That's the extent of the burn. The engine will go down after that, we won't be able to burn straight out again if there's trouble.
So what do you think? I'm not going to be a regular captain here. If you have a better idea, we need it.
Bethlehem Cross it is.
Course laid in, Captain.
Oh, fucking shut up, will you?

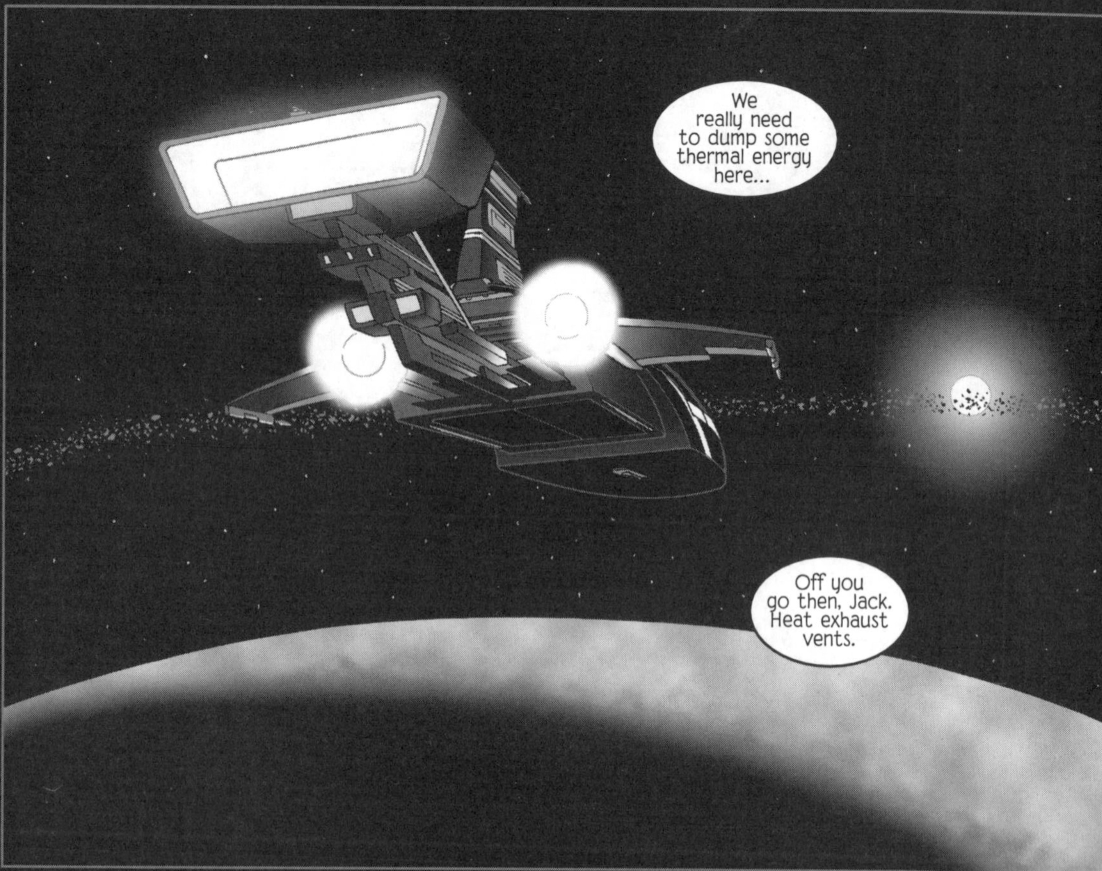
We really need to dump some thermal energy here...
Off you go then, Jack. Heat exhaust vents.

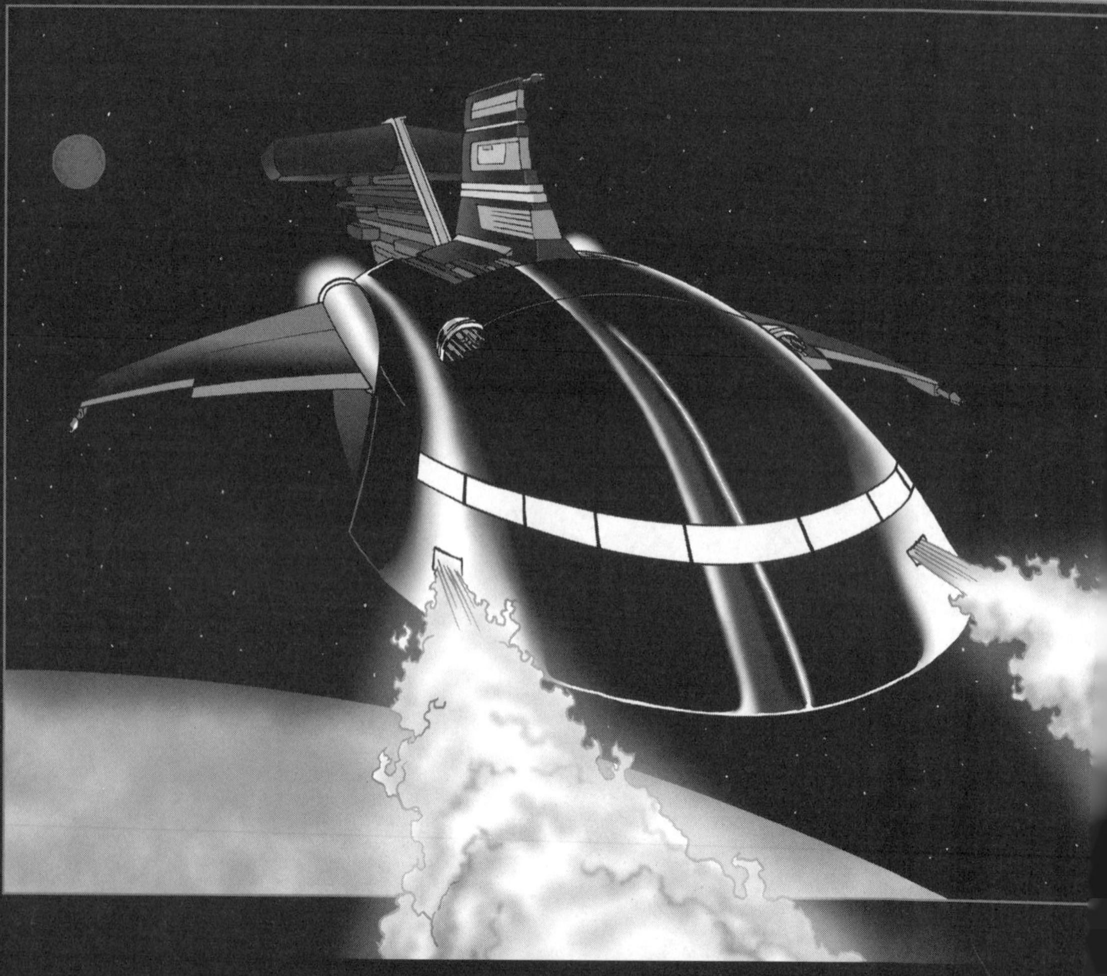

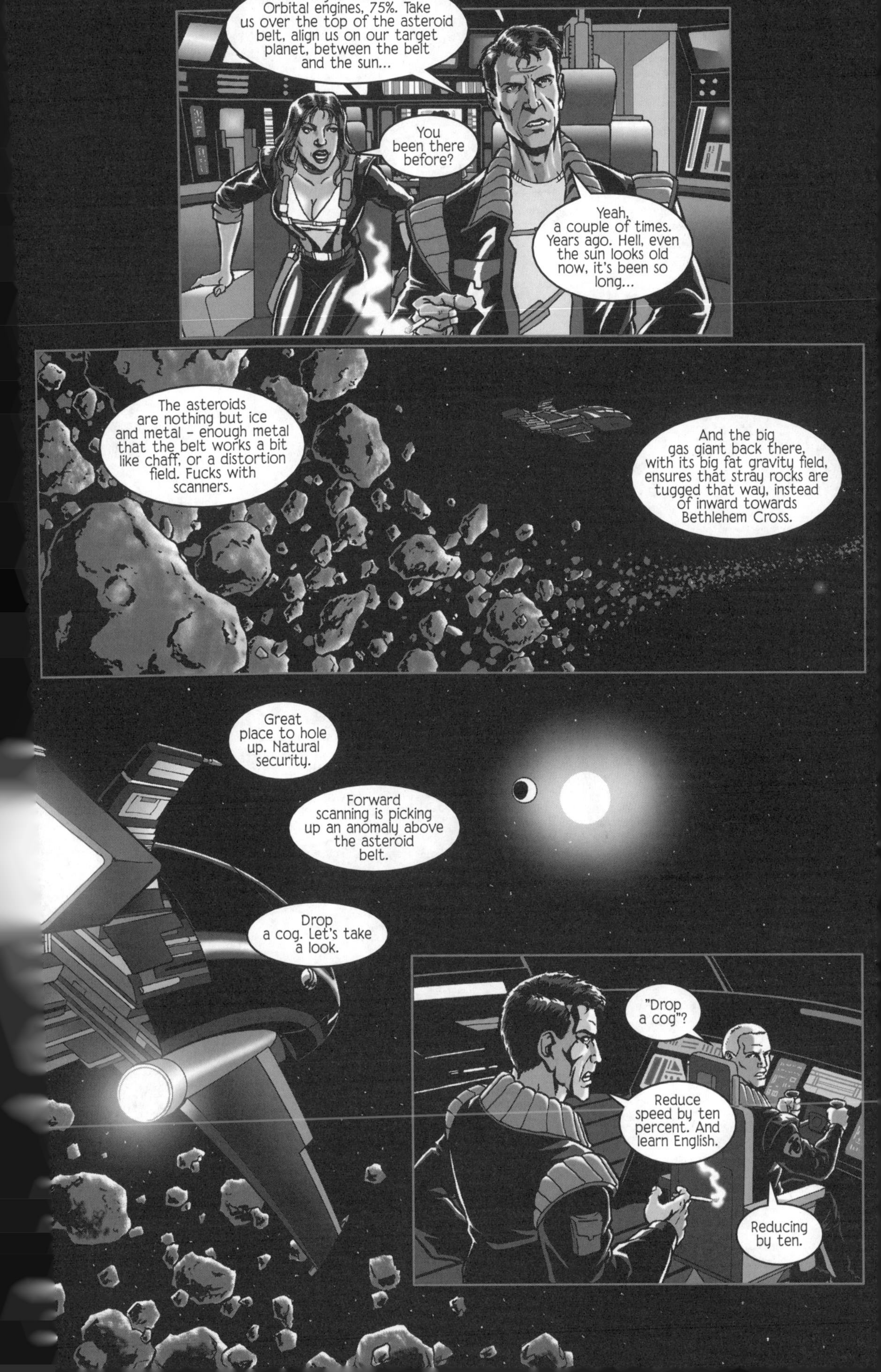
Right then. Orbital engines, 75%. Take us over the top of the asteroid belt, align us on our target planet, between the belt and the sun...
You been there before?
Yeah, a couple of times. Years ago. Hell, even the sun looks old now, it's been so long...
The asteroids are nothing but ice and metal - enough metal that the belt works a bit like chaff, or a distortion field. Fucks with scanners.
And the big gas giant back there, with its big fat gravity field, ensures that stray rocks are tugged that way, instead of inward towards Bethlehem Cross.
Great place to hole up. Natural security.
Forward scanning is picking up an anomaly above the asteroid belt.
Drop a cog. Let's take a look.
"Drop a cog"?
Reduce speed by ten percent. And learn English.
Reducing by ten.

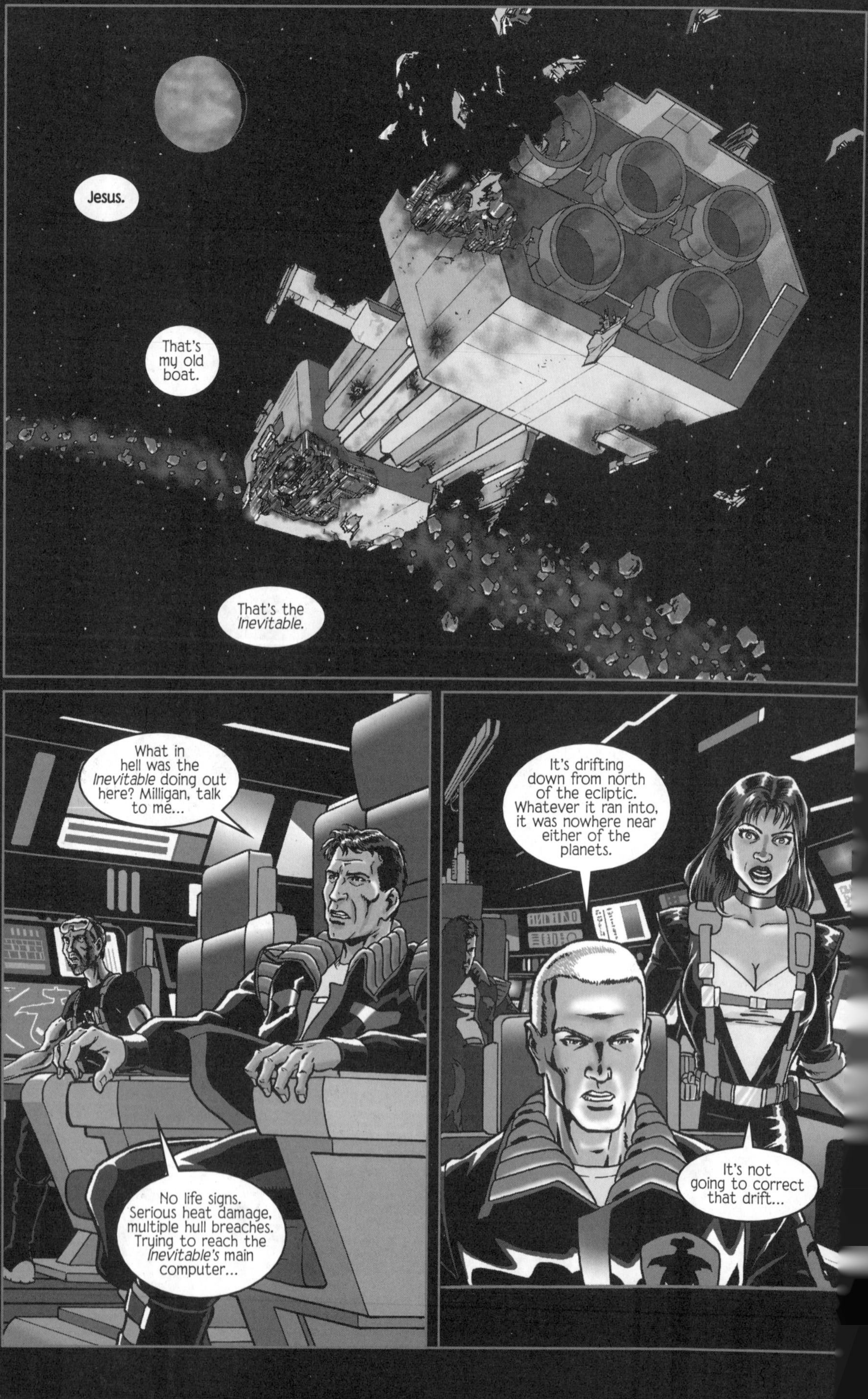

Jesus.
That's my old boat.
That's the *Inevitable.*
What in hell was the *Inevitable* doing out here? Milligan, talk to me...
No life signs. Serious heat damage, multiple hull breaches. Trying to reach the *Inevitable's* main computer...
It's drifting down from north of the ecliptic. Whatever it ran into, it was nowhere near either of the planets.
It's not going to correct that drift...

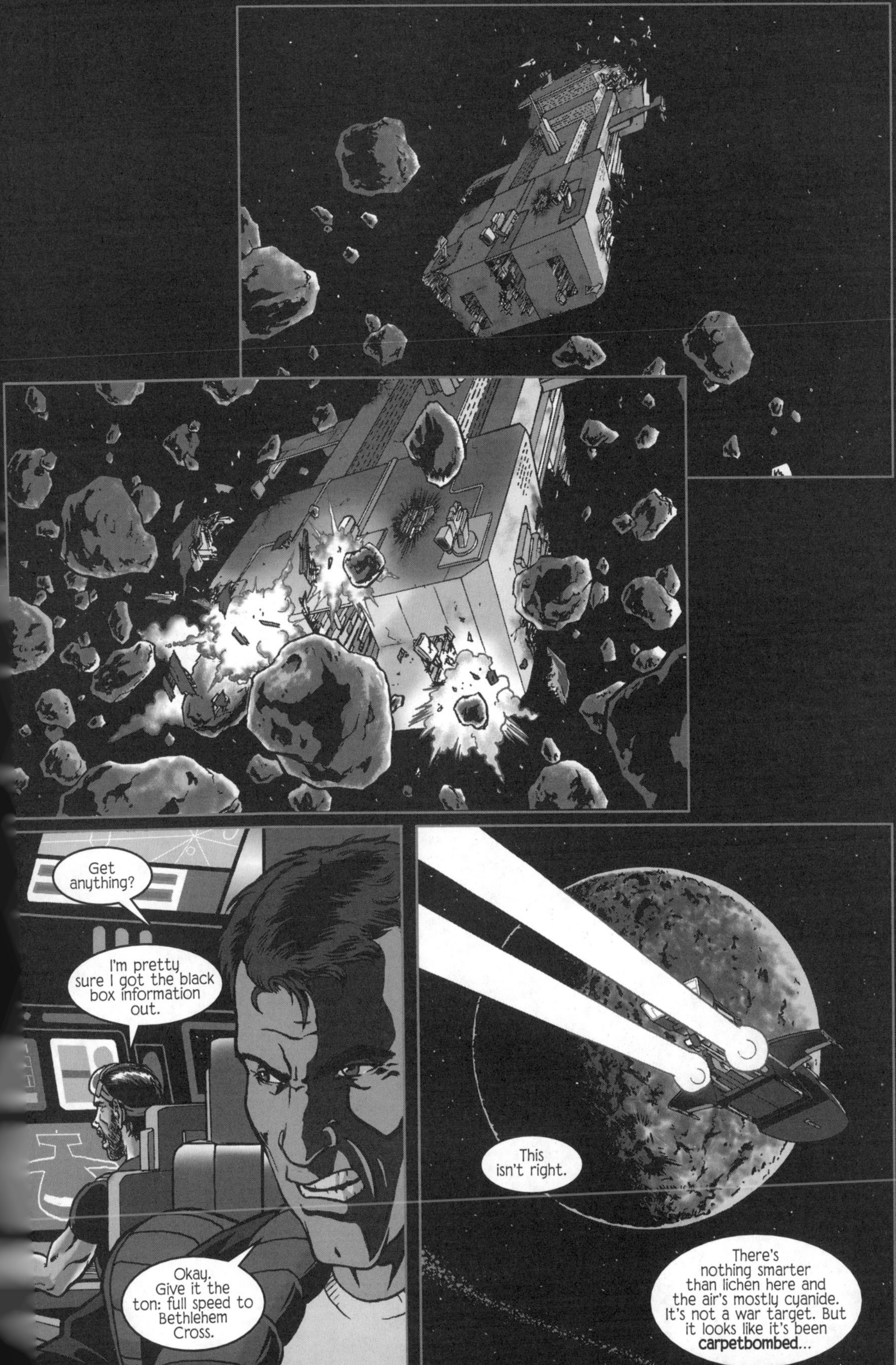
Get anything?
I'm pretty sure I got the black box information out.
Okay. Give it the ton: full speed to Bethlehem Cross.
This isn't right.
There's nothing smarter than lichen here and the air's mostly cyanide. It's not a war target. But it looks like it's been **carpetbombed**...

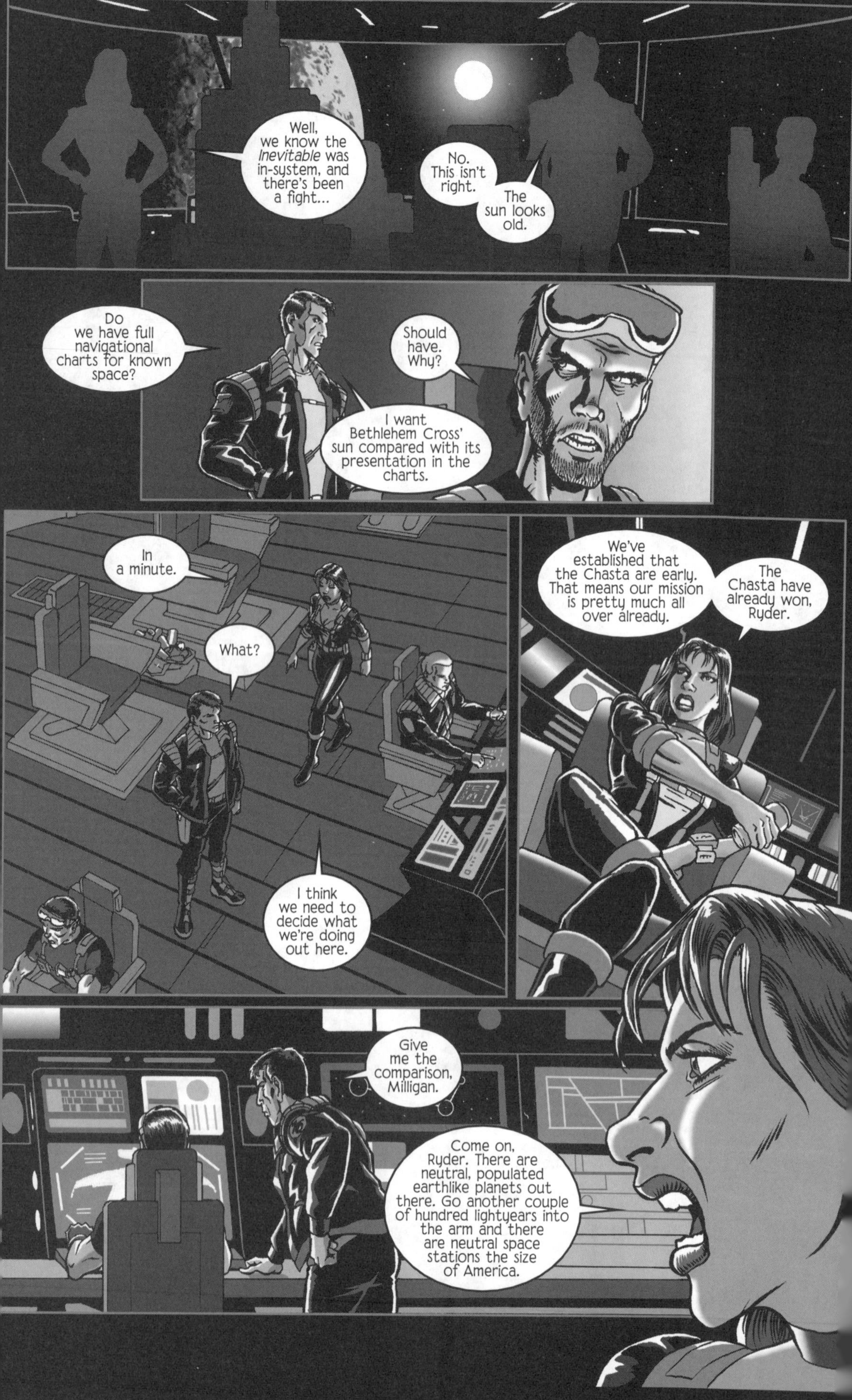

Well, we know the *Inevitable* was in-system, and there's been a fight...
No. This isn't right.
The sun looks old.
Do we have full navigational charts for known space?
Should have. Why?
I want Bethlehem Cross' sun compared with its presentation in the charts.
In a minute.
What?
I think we need to decide what we're doing out here.
We've established that the Chasta are early. That means our mission is pretty much all over already.
The Chasta have already won, Ryder.
Give me the comparison, Milligan.
Come on, Ryder. There are neutral, populated earthlike planets out there. Go another couple of hundred lightyears into the arm and there are neutral space stations the size of America.

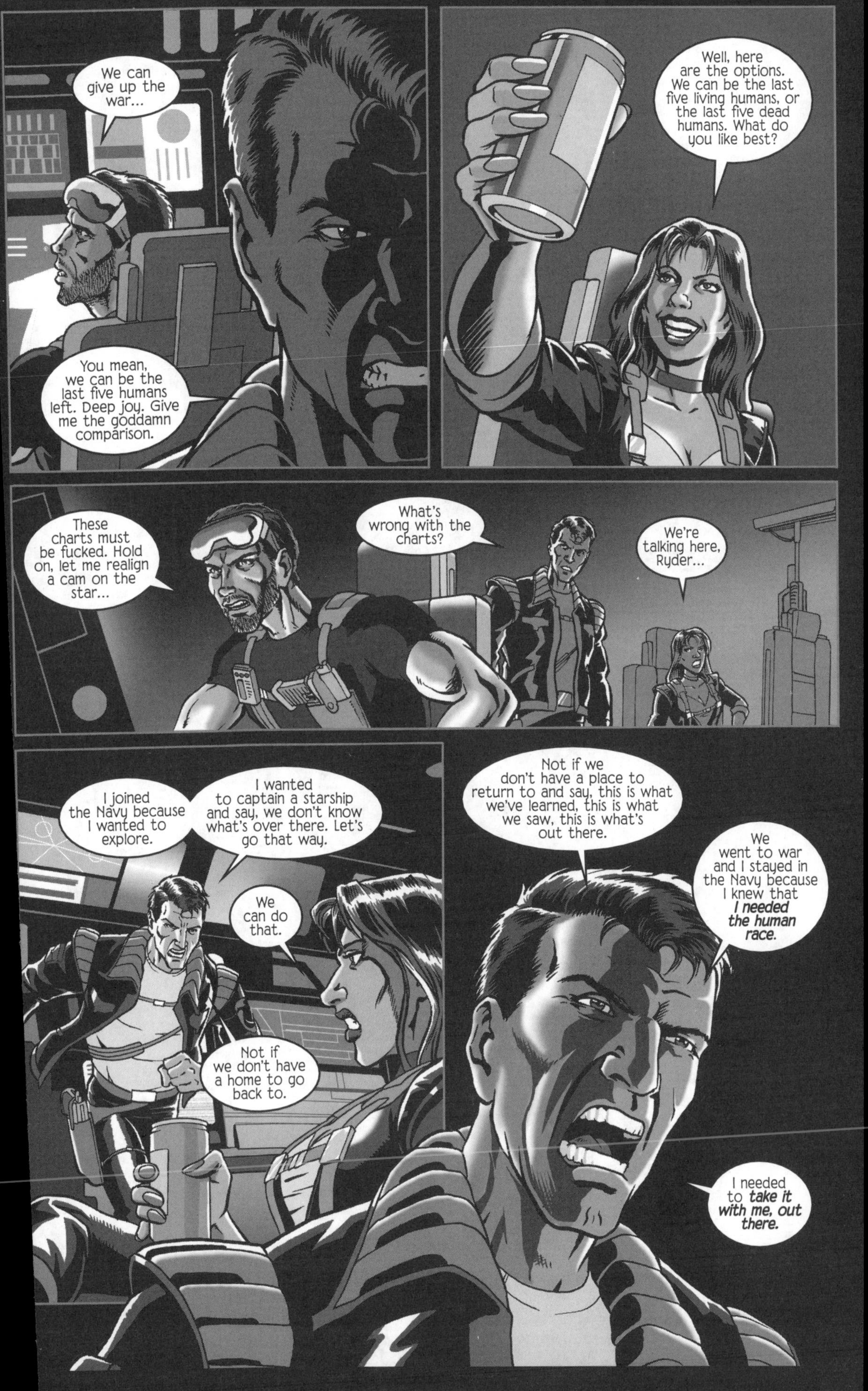

We can give up the war...
You mean, we can be the last five humans left. Deep joy. Give me the goddamn comparison.
Well, here are the options. We can be the last five living humans, or the last five dead humans. What do you like best?
These charts must be fucked. Hold on, let me realign a cam on the star...
What's wrong with the charts?
We're talking here, Ryder...
I joined the Navy because I wanted to explore.
I wanted to captain a starship and say, we don't know what's over there. Let's go that way.
We can do that.
Not if we don't have a home to go back to.
Not if we don't have a place to return to and say, this is what we've learned, this is what we saw, this is what's out there.
We went to war and I stayed in the Navy because I knew that ***I needed the human race.***
I needed to ***take it with me, out there.***

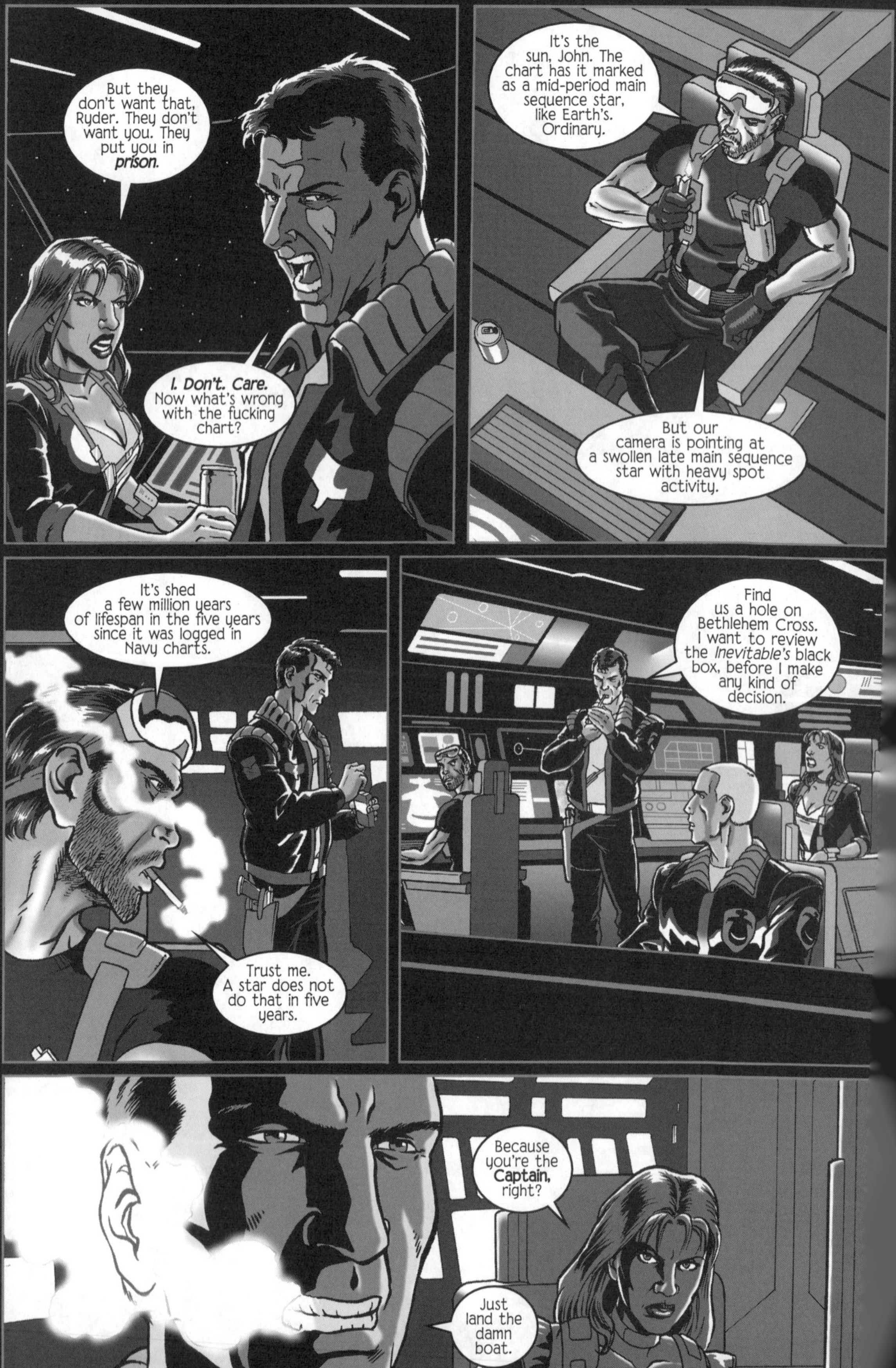

But they don't want that, Ryder. They don't want you. They put you in *prison*.
I. Don't. Care. Now what's wrong with the fucking chart?
It's the sun, John. The chart has it marked as a mid-period main sequence star, like Earth's. Ordinary.
But our camera is pointing at a swollen late main sequence star with heavy spot activity.
It's shed a few million years of lifespan in the five years since it was logged in Navy charts.
Trust me. A star does not do that in five years.
Find us a hole on Bethlehem Cross. I want to review the *Inevitable's* black box, before I make any kind of decision.
Because you're the **Captain,** right?
Just land the damn boat.

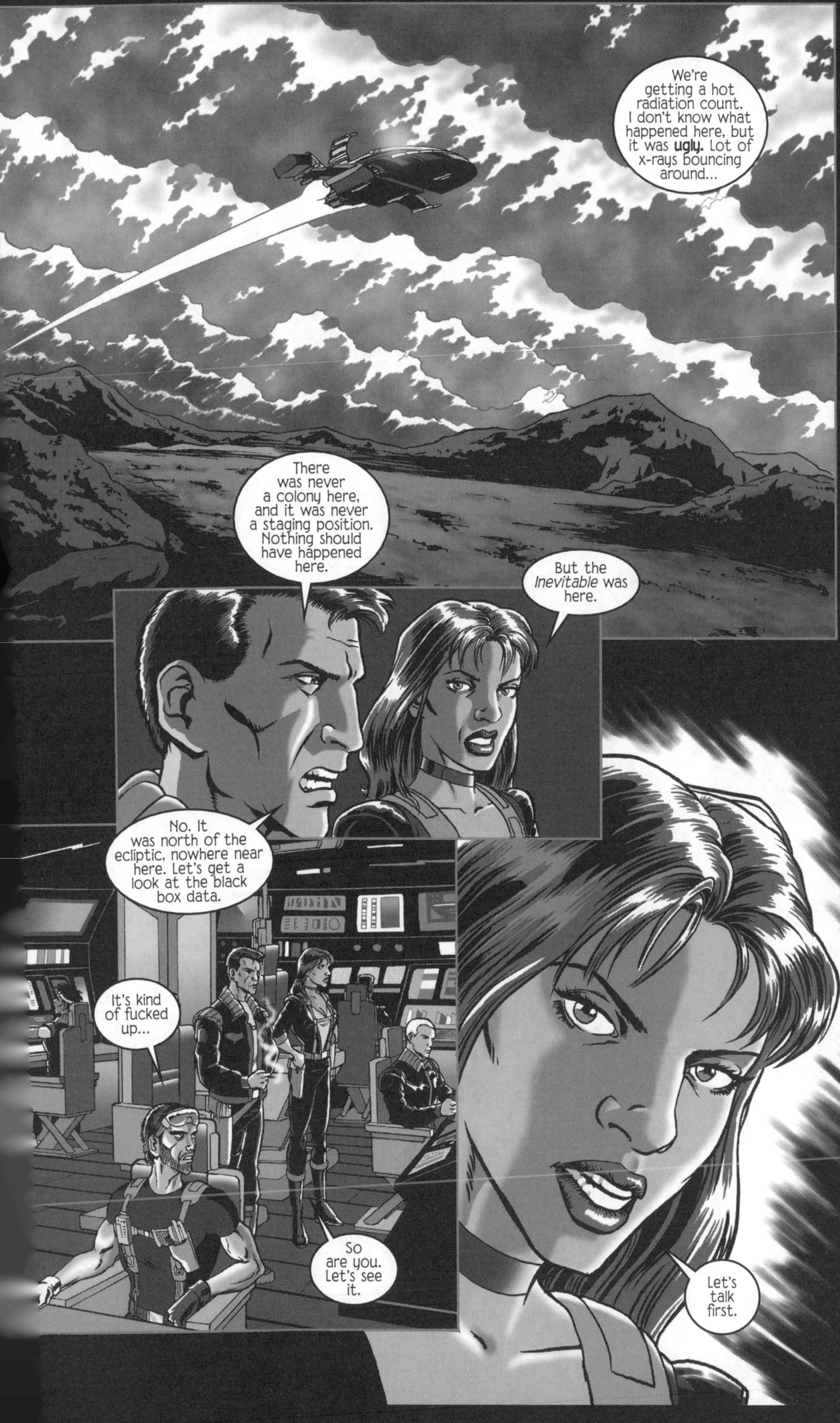
We're getting a hot radiation count. I don't know what happened here, but it was **ugly.** Lot of x-rays bouncing around...
There was never a colony here, and it was never a staging position. Nothing should have happened here.
But the *Inevitable* was here.
No. It was north of the ecliptic, nowhere near here. Let's get a look at the black box data.
It's kind of fucked up...
So are you. Let's see it.
Let's talk first.

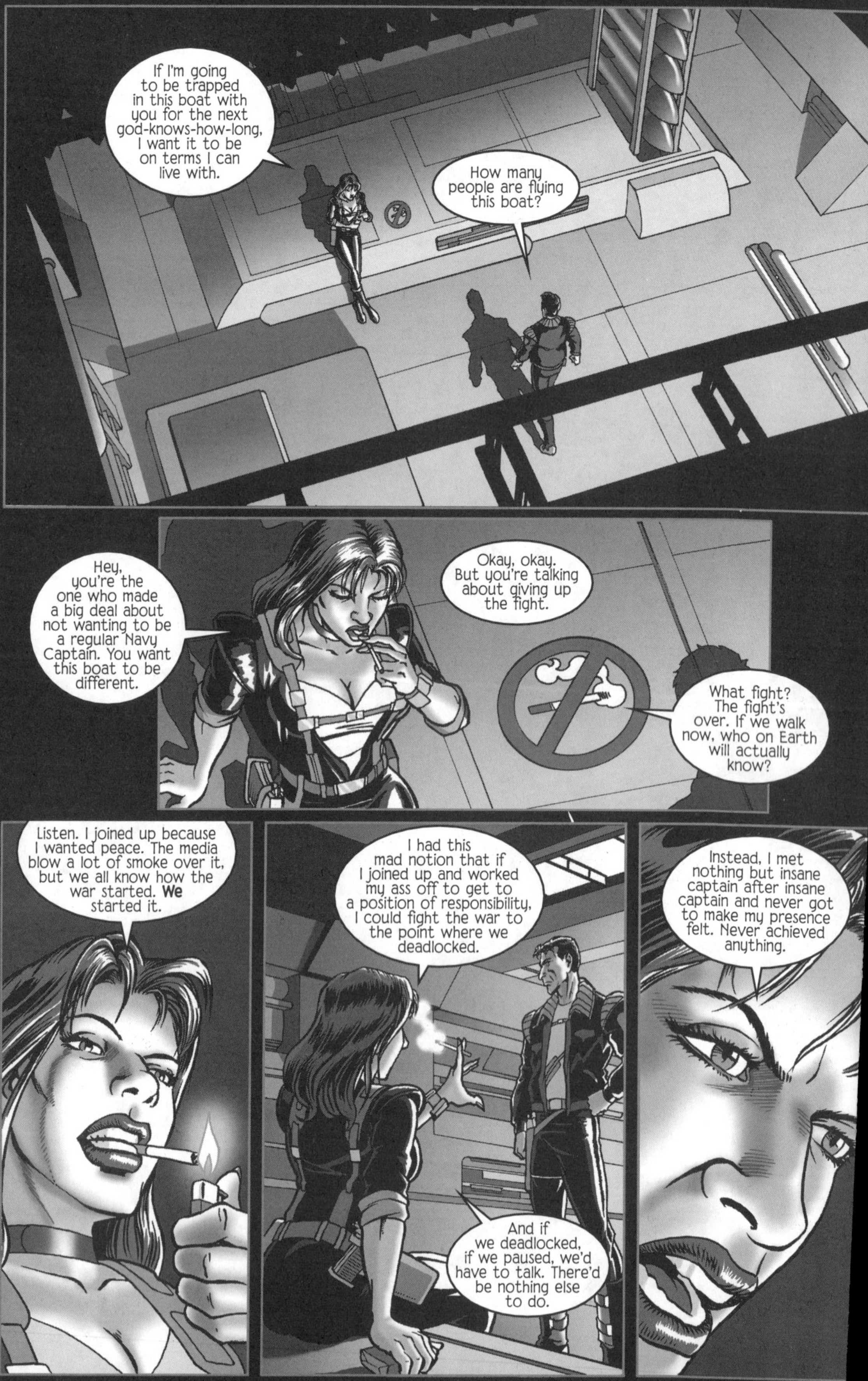

If I'm going to be trapped in this boat with you for the next god-knows-how-long, I want it to be on terms I can live with.
How many people are flying this boat?
Hey, you're the one who made a big deal about not wanting to be a regular Navy Captain. You want this boat to be different.
Okay, okay. But you're talking about giving up the fight.
What fight? The fight's over. If we walk now, who on Earth will actually know?
Listen. I joined up because I wanted peace. The media blow a lot of smoke over it, but we all know how the war started. **We** started it.
I had this mad notion that if I joined up and worked my ass off to get to a position of responsibility, I could fight the war to the point where we deadlocked.
And if we deadlocked, if we paused, we'd have to talk. There'd be nothing else to do.
Instead, I met nothing but insane captain after insane captain and never got to make my presence felt. Never achieved anything.

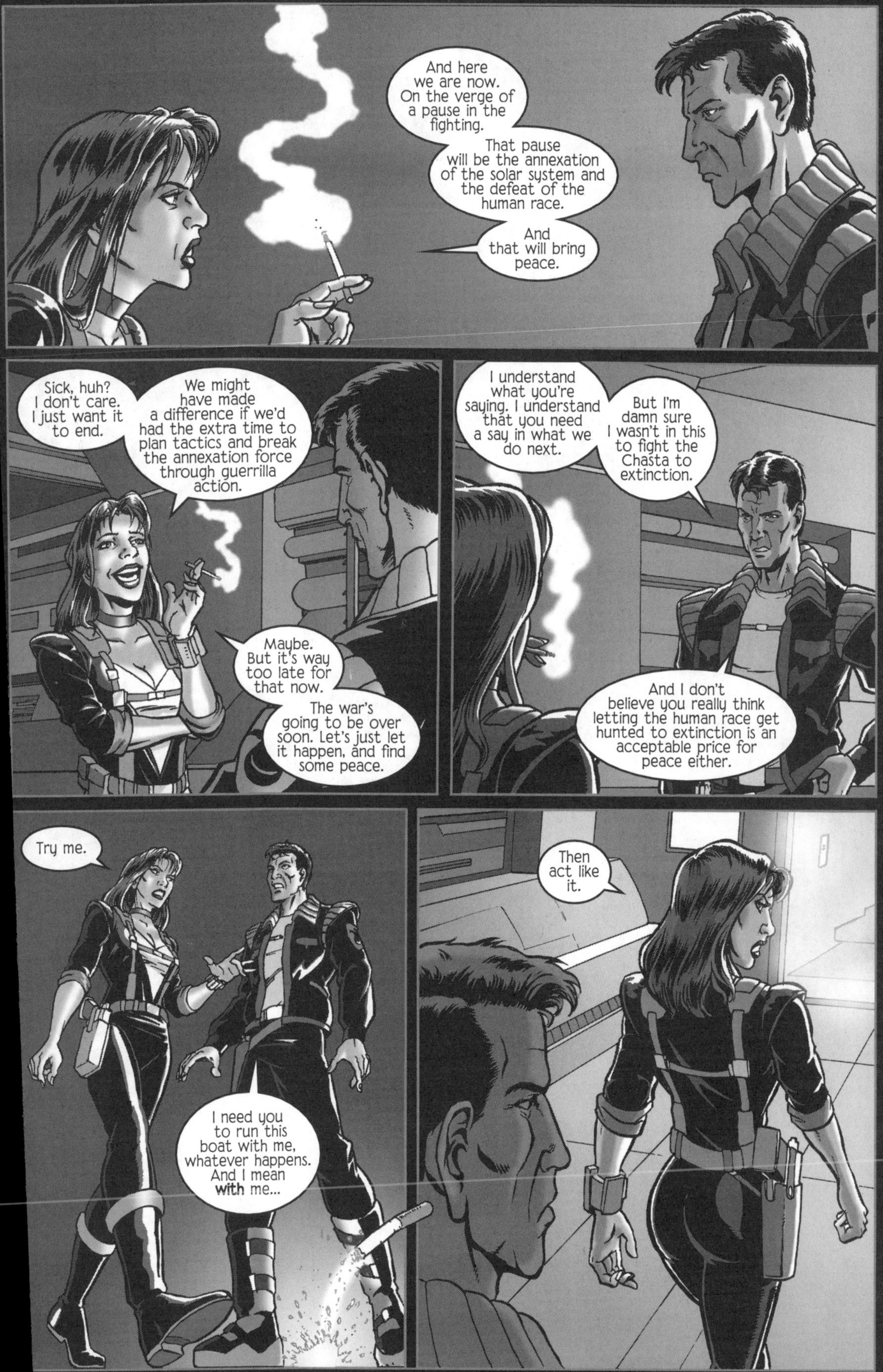
And here we are now. On the verge of a pause in the fighting.
That pause will be the annexation of the solar system and the defeat of the human race.
And that will bring peace.
Sick, huh? I don't care. I just want it to end.
We might have made a difference if we'd had the extra time to plan tactics and break the annexation force through guerrilla action.
Maybe. But it's way too late for that now.
The war's going to be over soon. Let's just let it happen, and find some peace.
I understand what you're saying. I understand that you need a say in what we do next.
But I'm damn sure I wasn't in this to fight the Chasta to extinction.
And I don't believe you really think letting the human race get hunted to extinction is an acceptable price for peace either.
Try me.
I need you to run this boat with me, whatever happens. And I mean **with** me...
Then act like it.

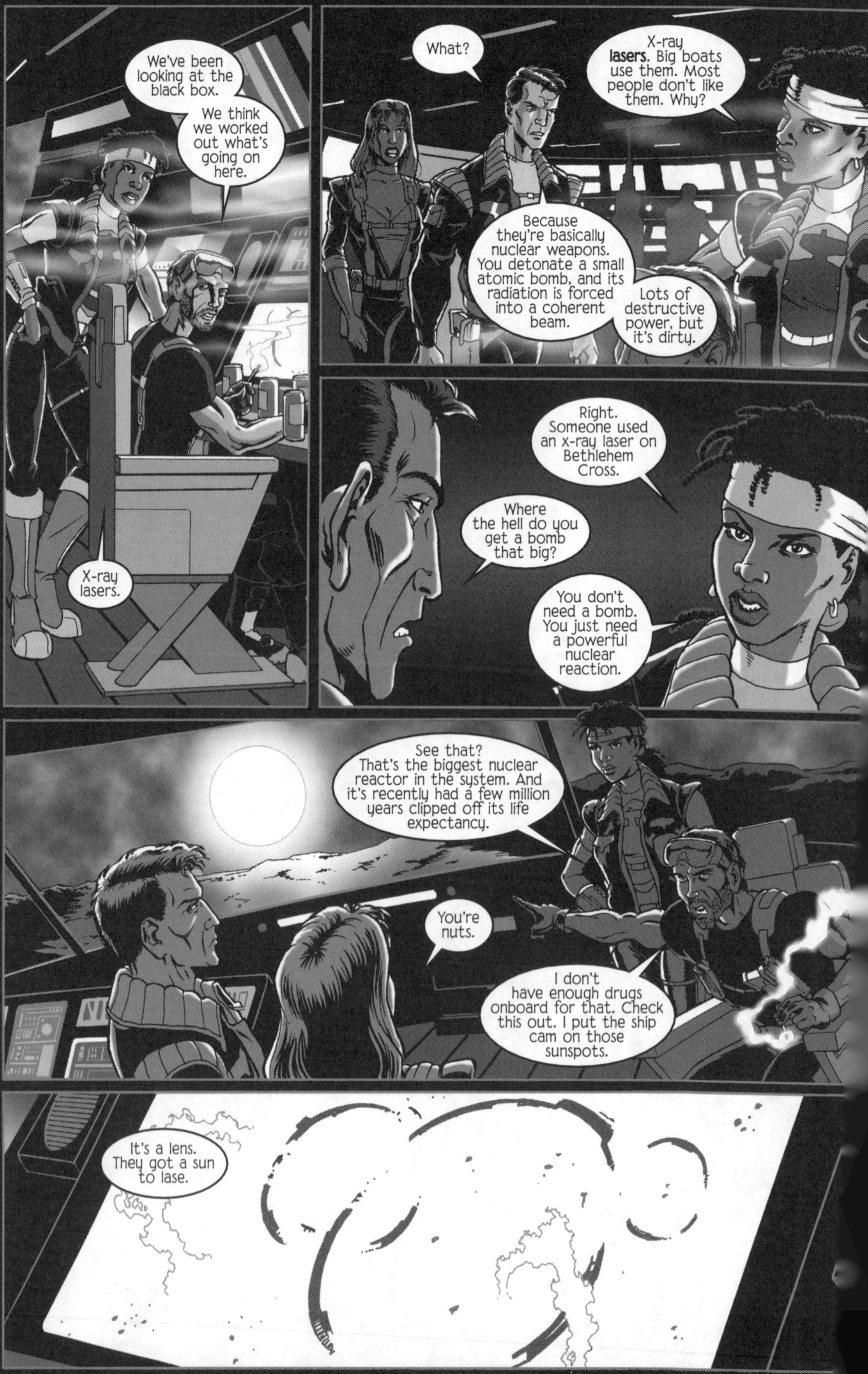
We've been looking at the black box.
We think we worked out what's going on here.
X-ray lasers.
What?
X-ray **lasers**. Big boats use them. Most people don't like them. Why?
Because they're basically nuclear weapons. You detonate a small atomic bomb, and its radiation is forced into a coherent beam.
Lots of destructive power, but it's dirty.
Right. Someone used an x-ray laser on Bethlehem Cross.
Where the hell do you get a bomb that big?
You don't need a bomb. You just need a powerful nuclear reaction.
See that? That's the biggest nuclear reactor in the system. And it's recently had a few million years clipped off its life expectancy.
You're nuts.
I don't have enough drugs onboard for that. Check this out. I put the ship cam on those sunspots.
It's a lens. They got a sun to lase.

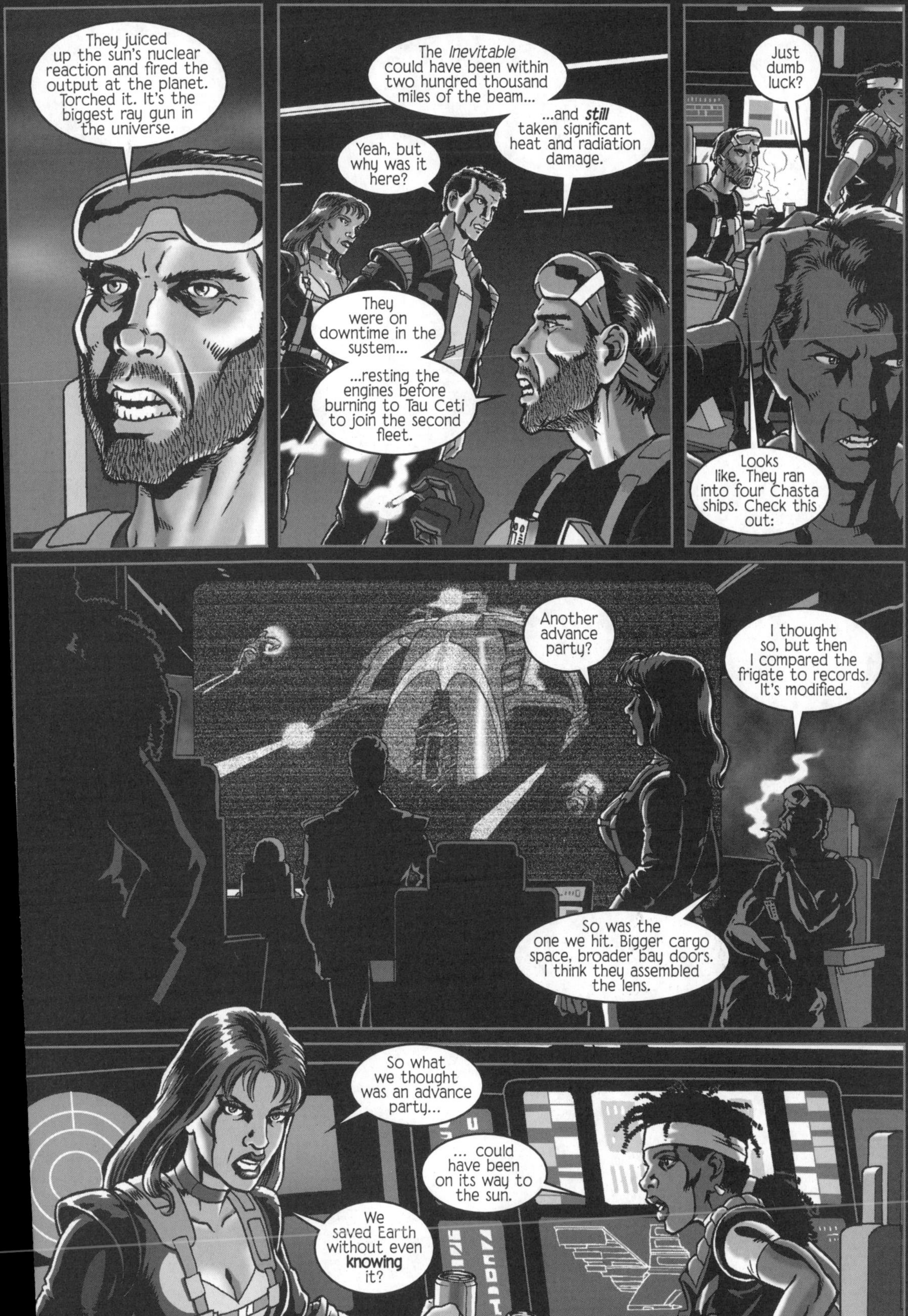
They juiced up the sun's nuclear reaction and fired the output at the planet. Torched it. It's the biggest ray gun in the universe.
The *Inevitable* could have been within two hundred thousand miles of the beam...
...and ***still*** taken significant heat and radiation damage.
Yeah, but why was it here?
They were on downtime in the system...
...resting the engines before burning to Tau Ceti to join the second fleet.
Just dumb luck?
Looks like. They ran into four Chasta ships. Check this out:
Another advance party?
I thought so, but then I compared the frigate to records. It's modified.
So was the one we hit. Bigger cargo space, broader bay doors. I think they assembled the lens.
So what we thought was an advance party...
... could have been on its way to the sun.
We saved Earth without even **knowing** it?

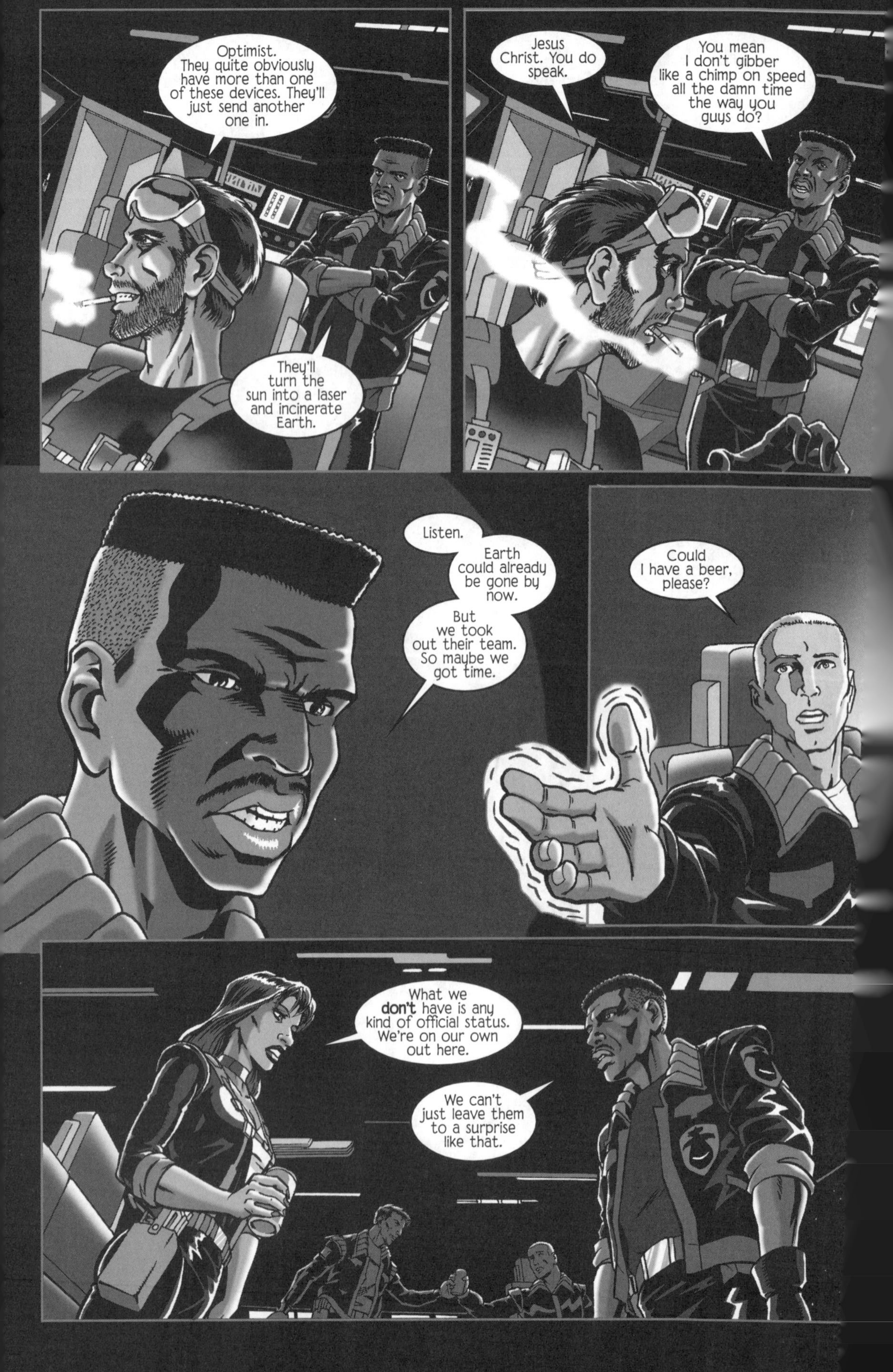
Optimist. They quite obviously have more than one of these devices. They'll just send another one in.
They'll turn the sun into a laser and incinerate Earth.
Jesus Christ. You do speak.
You mean I don't gibber like a chimp on speed all the damn time the way you guys do?
Listen.
Earth could already be gone by now.
But we took out their team. So maybe we got time.
Could I have a beer, please?
What we don't have is any kind of official status. We're on our own out here.
We can't just leave them to a surprise like that.

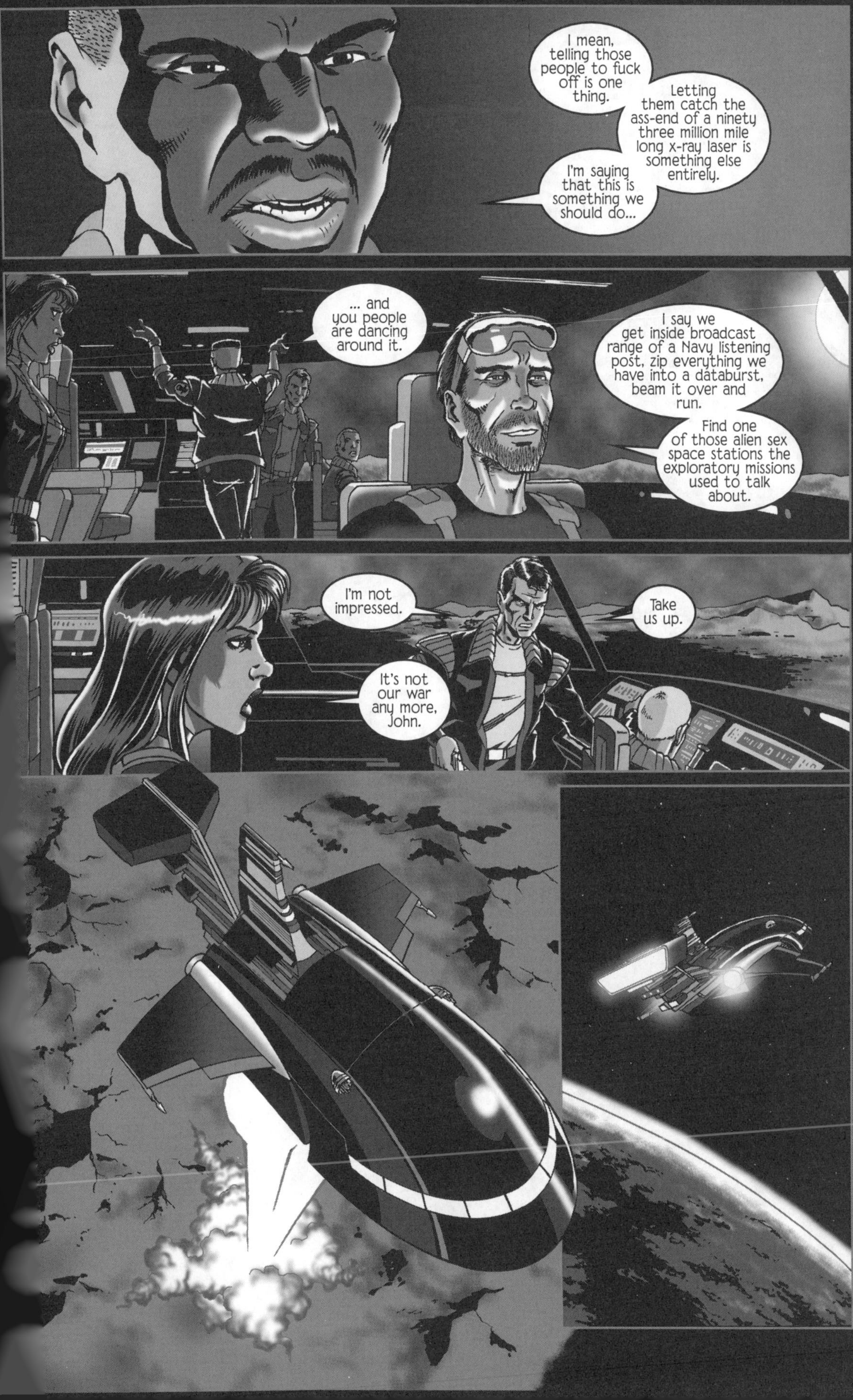
I mean, telling those people to fuck off is one thing.
Letting them catch the ass-end of a ninety three million mile long x-ray laser is something else entirely.
I'm saying that this is something we should do...
... and you people are dancing around it.
I say we get inside broadcast range of a Navy listening post, zip everything we have into a databurst, beam it over and run.
Find one of those alien sex space stations the exploratory missions used to talk about.
I'm not impressed.
It's not our war any more, John.
Take us up.

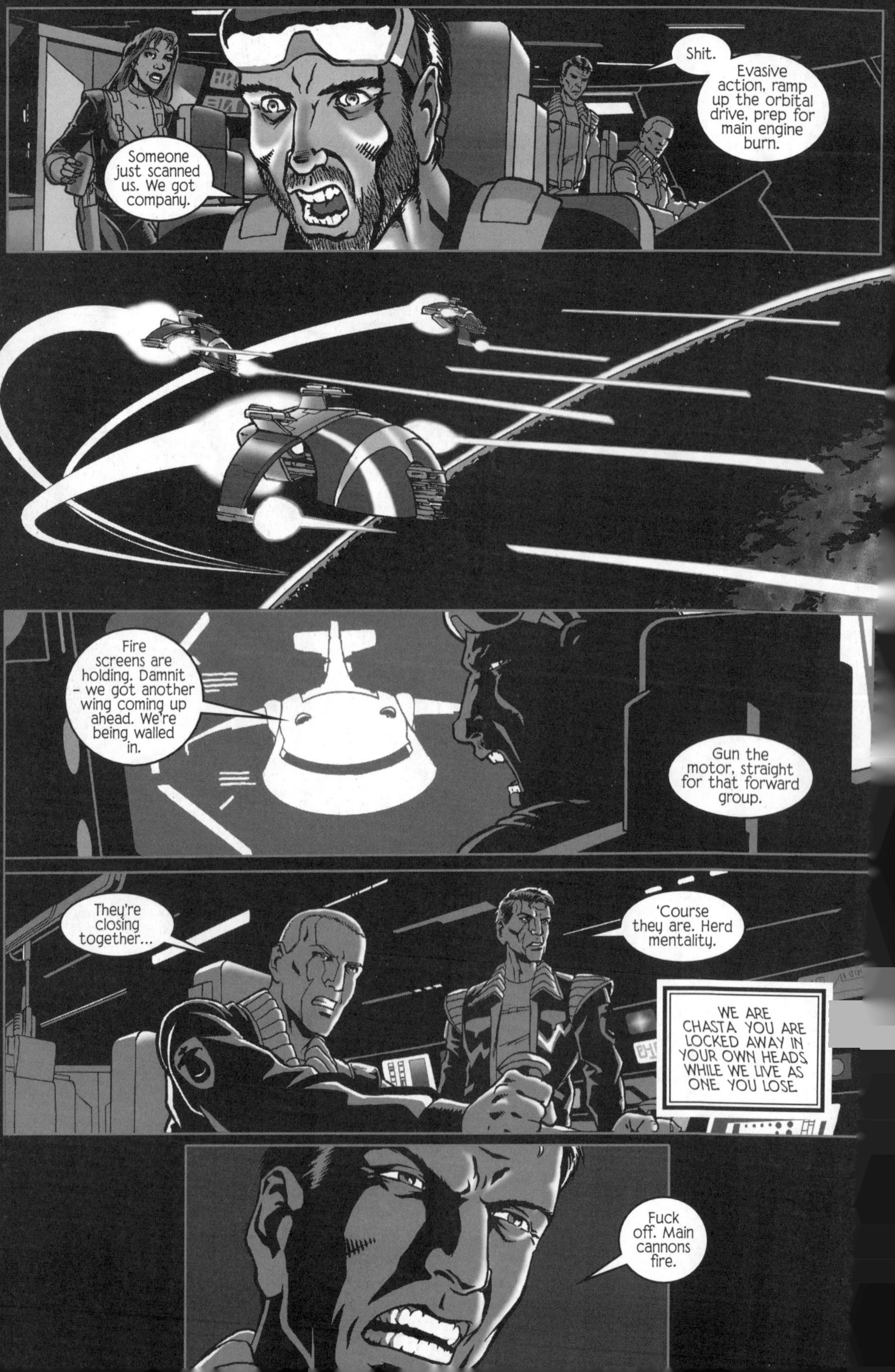

Someone just scanned us. We got company.
Shit.
Evasive action, ramp up the orbital drive, prep for main engine burn.
Fire screens are holding. Damnit - we got another wing coming up ahead. We're being walled in.
Gun the motor, straight for that forward group.
They're closing together...
'Course they are. Herd mentality.
WE ARE CHASTA. YOU ARE LOCKED AWAY IN YOUR OWN HEADS, WHILE WE LIVE AS ONE. YOU LOSE.
Fuck off. Main cannons fire.

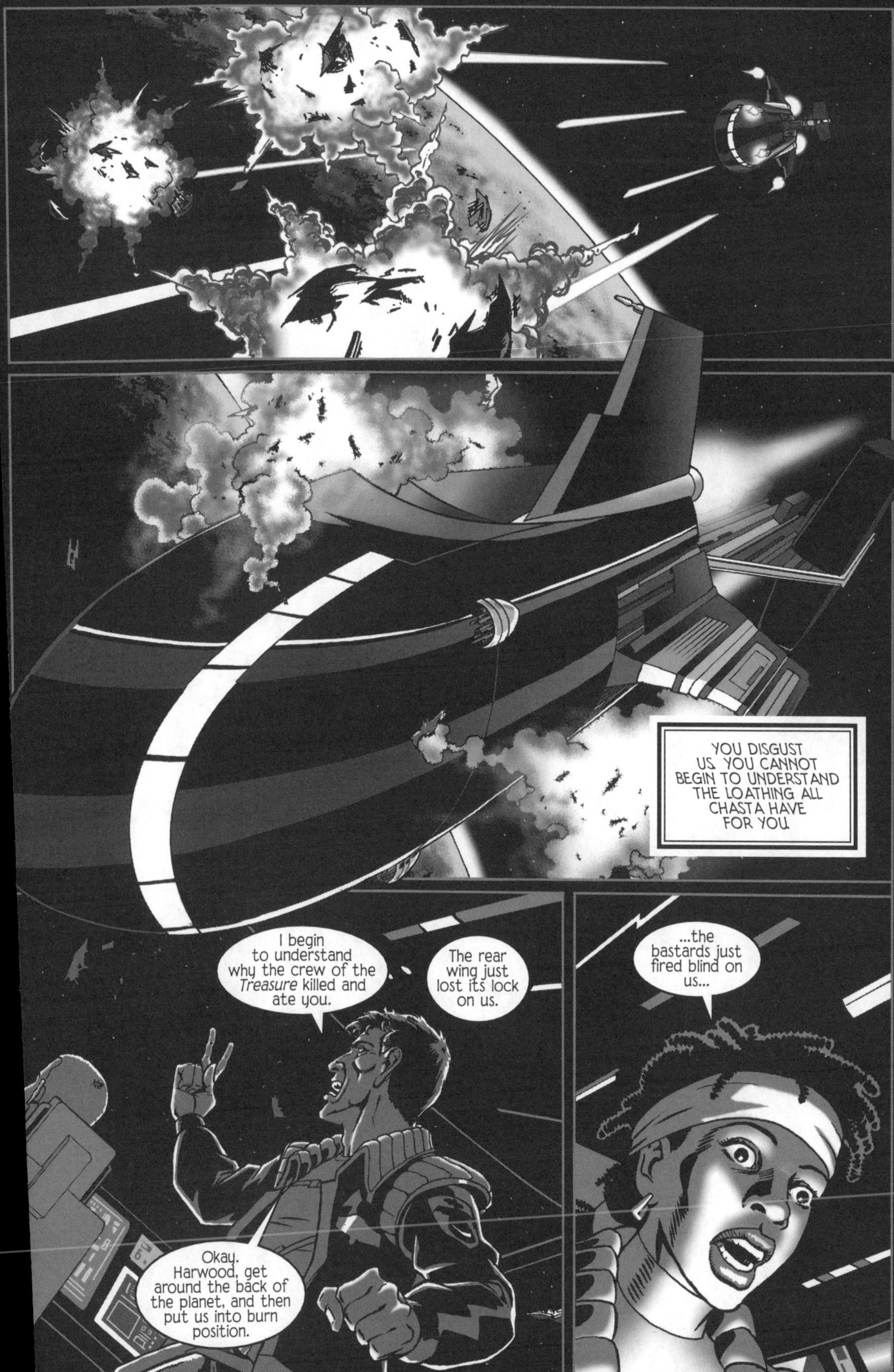
YOU DISGUST US. YOU CANNOT BEGIN TO UNDERSTAND THE LOATHING ALL CHASTA HAVE FOR YOU.
I begin to understand why the crew of the *Treasure* killed and ate you.
The rear wing just lost its lock on us.
Okay. Harwood, get around the back of the planet, and then put us into burn position.
...the bastards just fired blind on us...

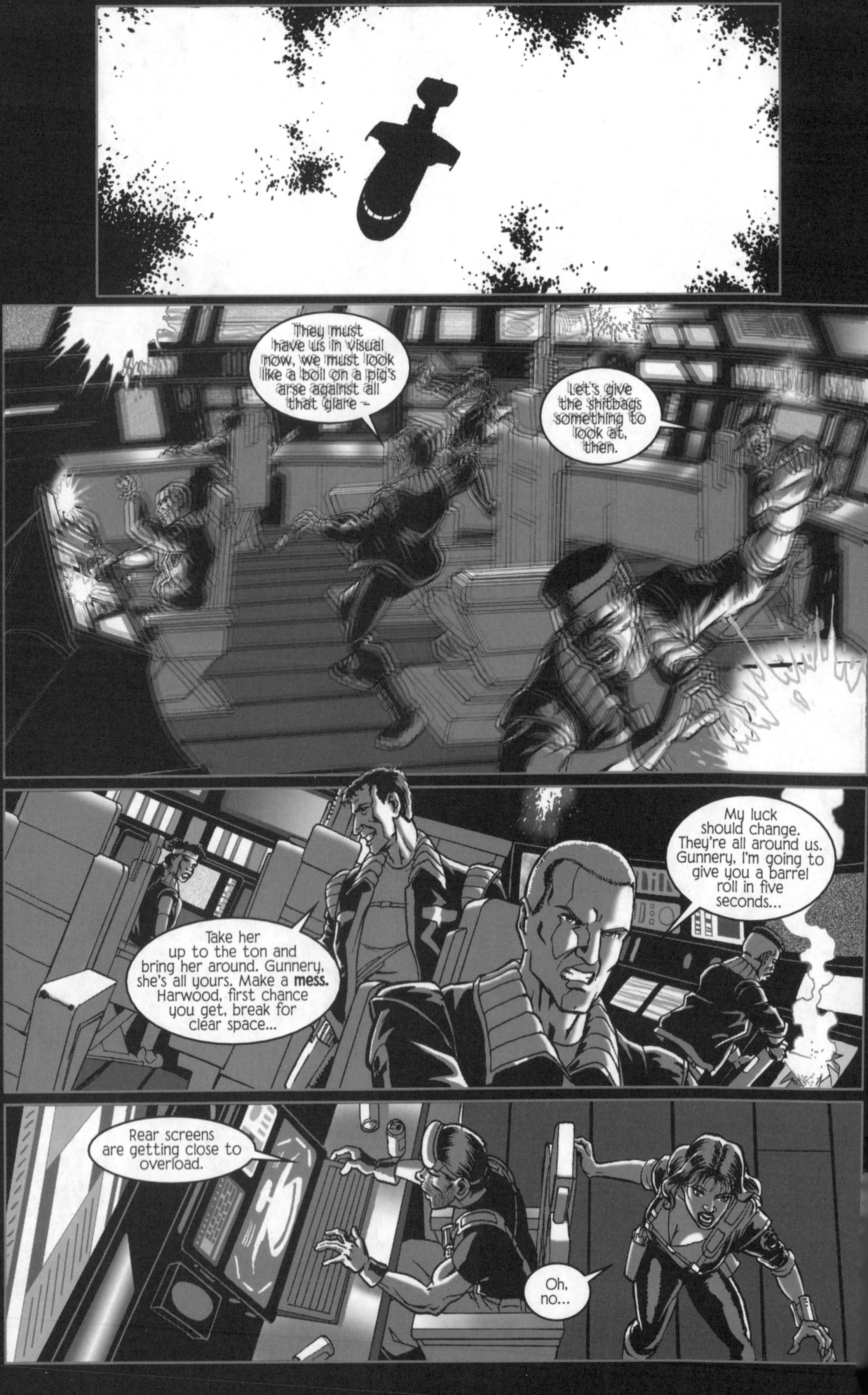
They must have us in visual now, we must look like a boil on a pig's arse against all that glare -
Let's give the shitbags something to look at, then.
Take her up to the ton and bring her around. Gunnery, she's all yours. Make a **mess.** Harwood, first chance you get, break for clear space...
My luck should change. They're all around us. Gunnery, I'm going to give you a barrel roll in five seconds...
Rear screens are getting close to overload.
Oh, no...

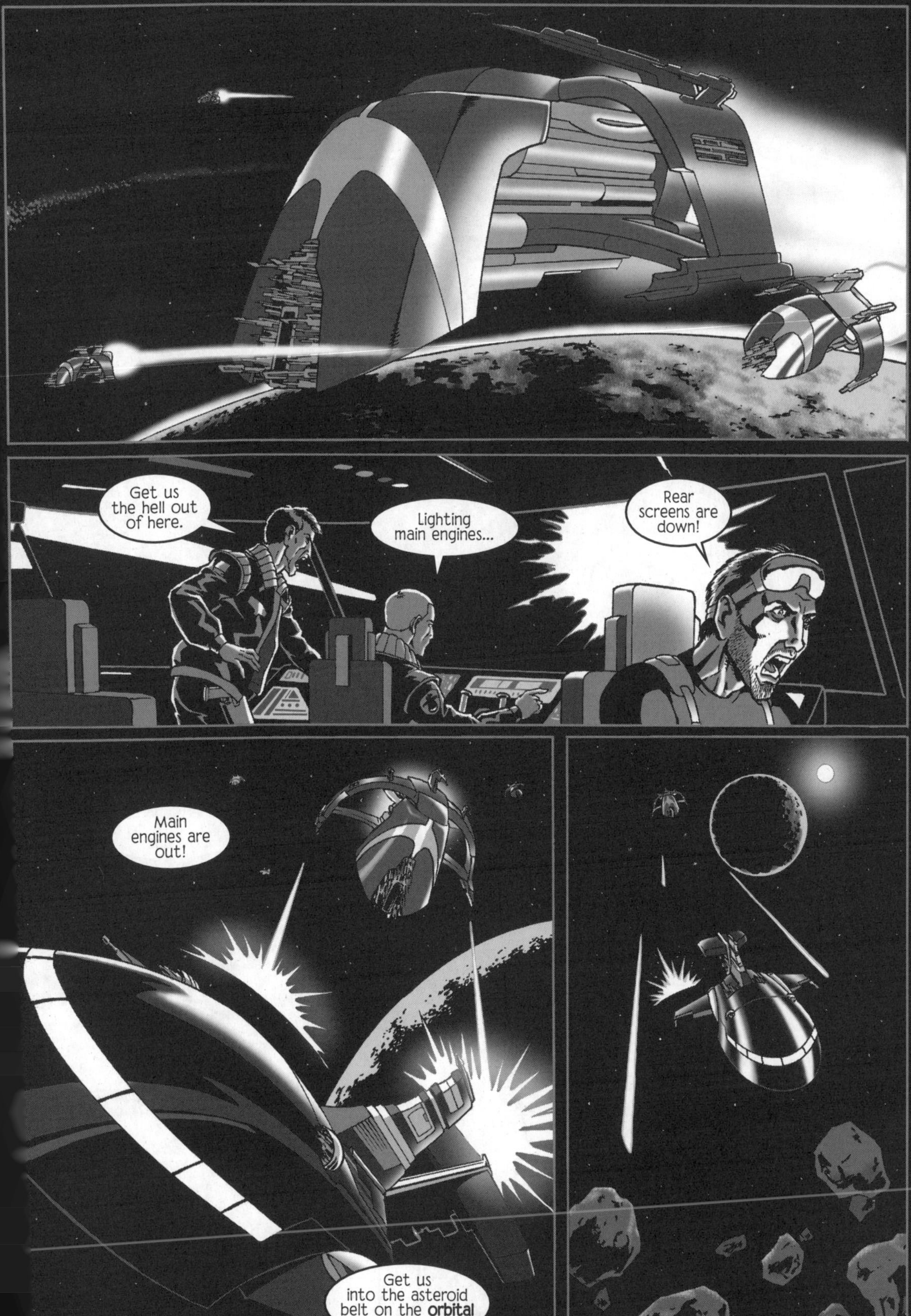

Get us the hell out of here.
Lighting main engines...
Rear screens are down!
Main engines are out!
Get us into the asteroid belt on the **orbital** engines!

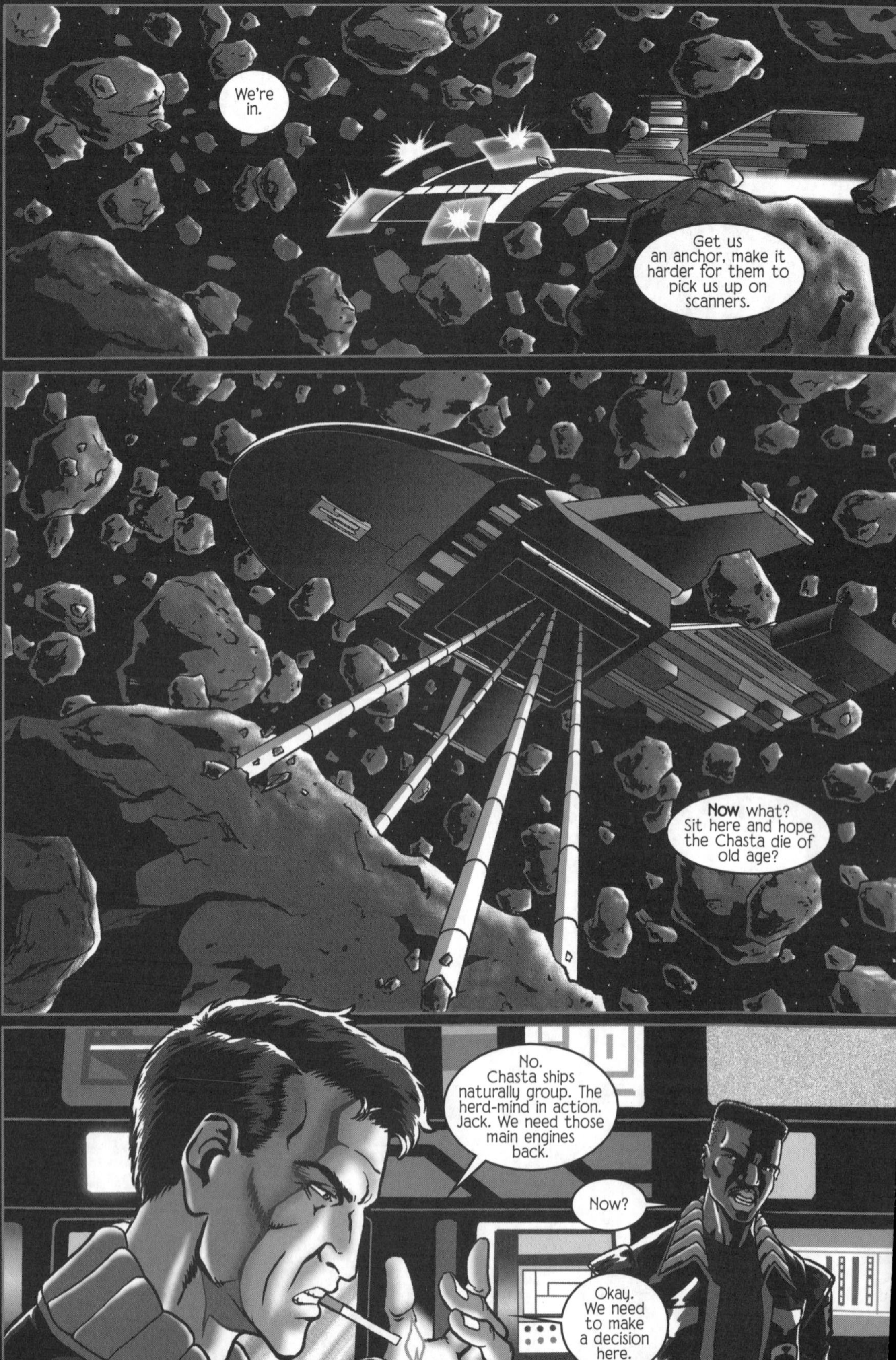
We're in.
Get us an anchor, make it harder for them to pick us up on scanners.
Now what? Sit here and hope the Chasta die of old age?
No. Chasta ships naturally group. The herd-mind in action. Jack. We need those main engines back.
Now?
Okay. We need to make a decision here.

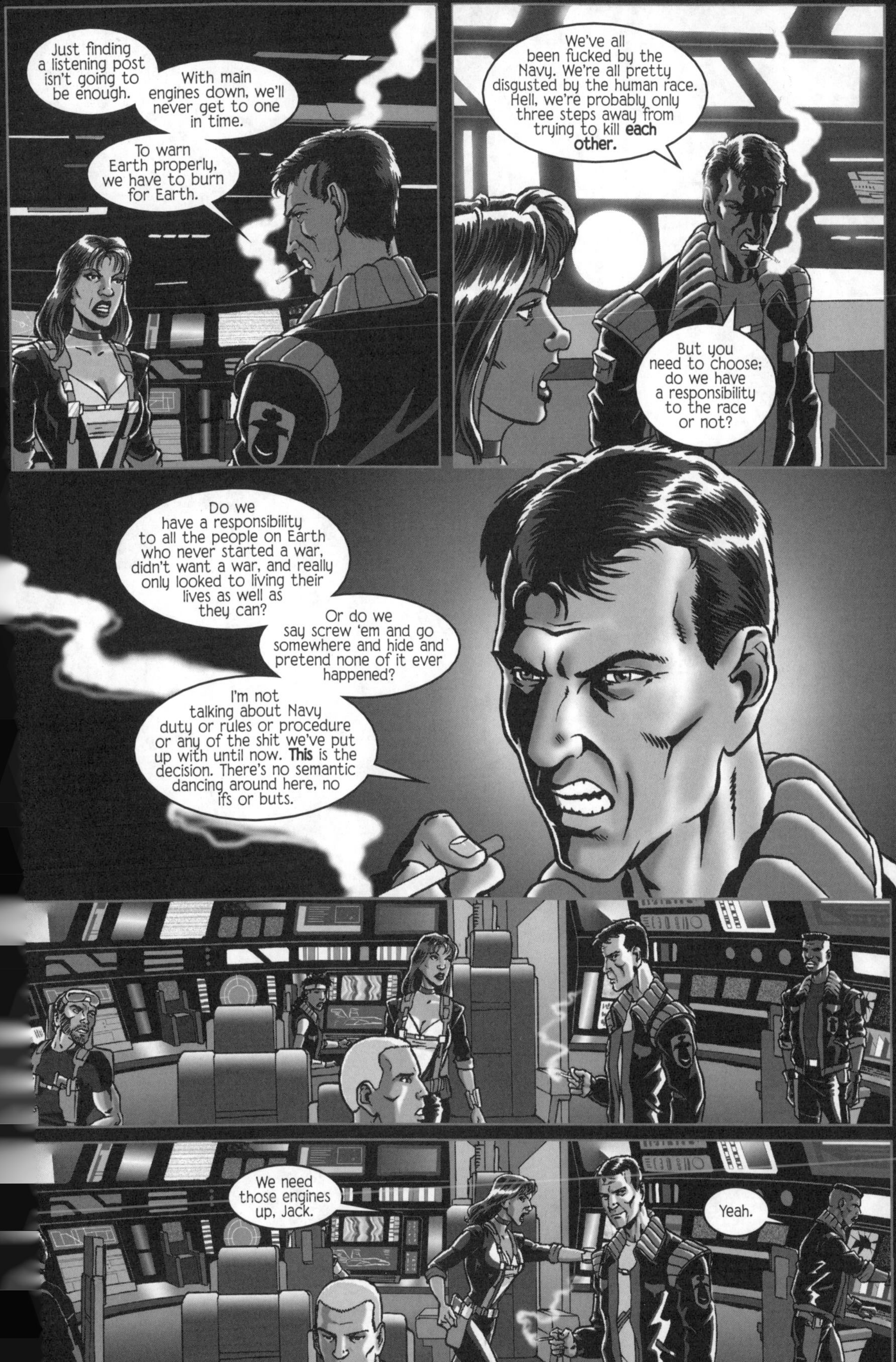
Just finding a listening post isn't going to be enough.
With main engines down, we'll never get to one in time.
To warn Earth properly, we have to burn for Earth.
We've all been fucked by the Navy. We're all pretty disgusted by the human race. Hell, we're probably only three steps away from trying to kill **each other.**
But you need to choose; do we have a responsibility to the race or not?
Do we have a responsibility to all the people on Earth who never started a war, didn't want a war, and really only looked to living their lives as well as they can?
Or do we say screw 'em and go somewhere and hide and pretend none of it ever happened?
I'm not talking about Navy duty or rules or procedure or any of the shit we've put up with until now. **This** is the decision. There's no semantic dancing around here, no ifs or buts.
We need those engines up, Jack.
Yeah.

Right. Aliya. I want a bit of precision work from you. These rocks are just ice and metal.

If you targeted an icy core with a laser, what do you think would happen?

Well... I'd break some ice? I dunno... the ice would evaporate, I suppose...

Right. And what would that do to the asteroid?

It'd move in the opposite direction from the outgassing a bit. Basic action/reaction stuff.

Right. I want to chuck big rocks at the Chasta.

And I want a location on the *Inevitable*. I got an idea.

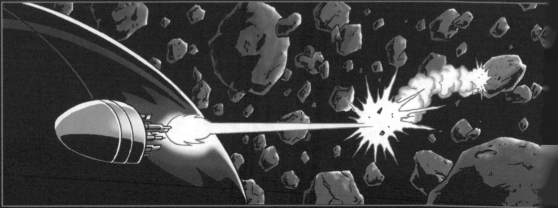

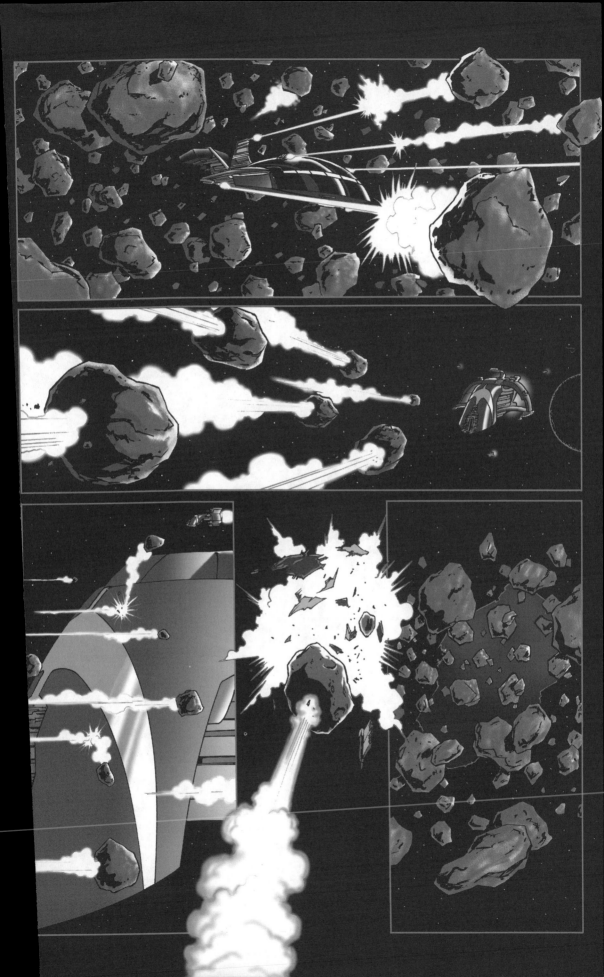

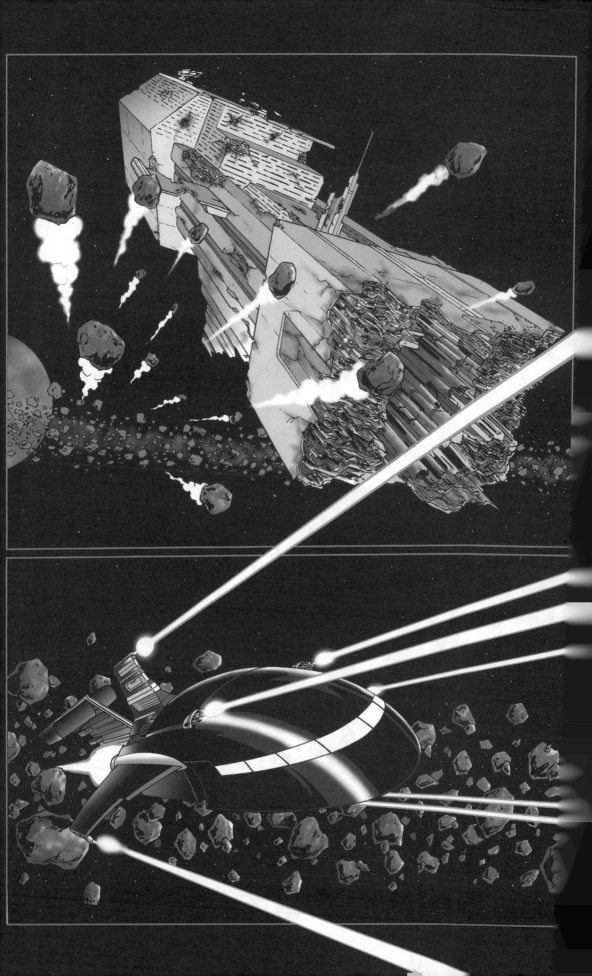

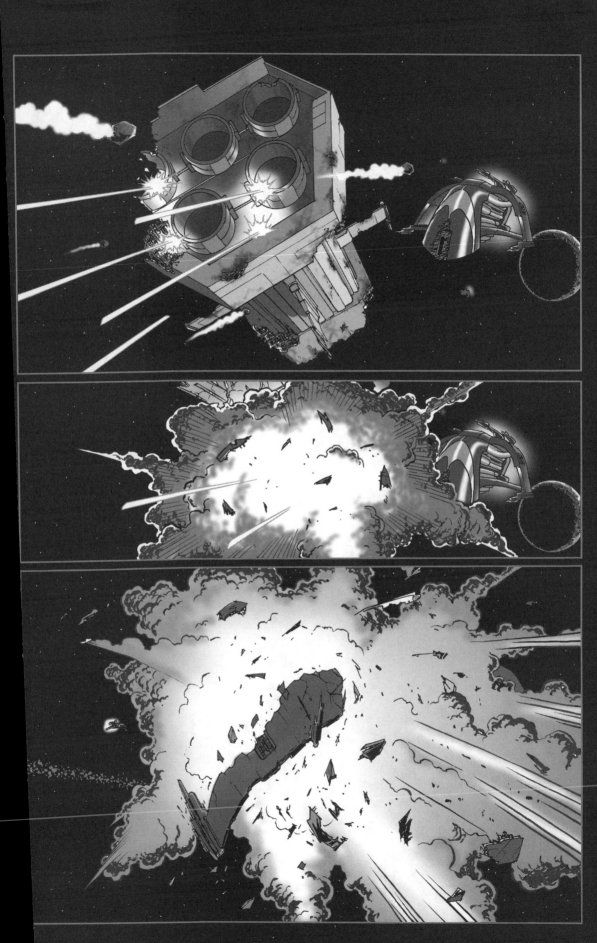

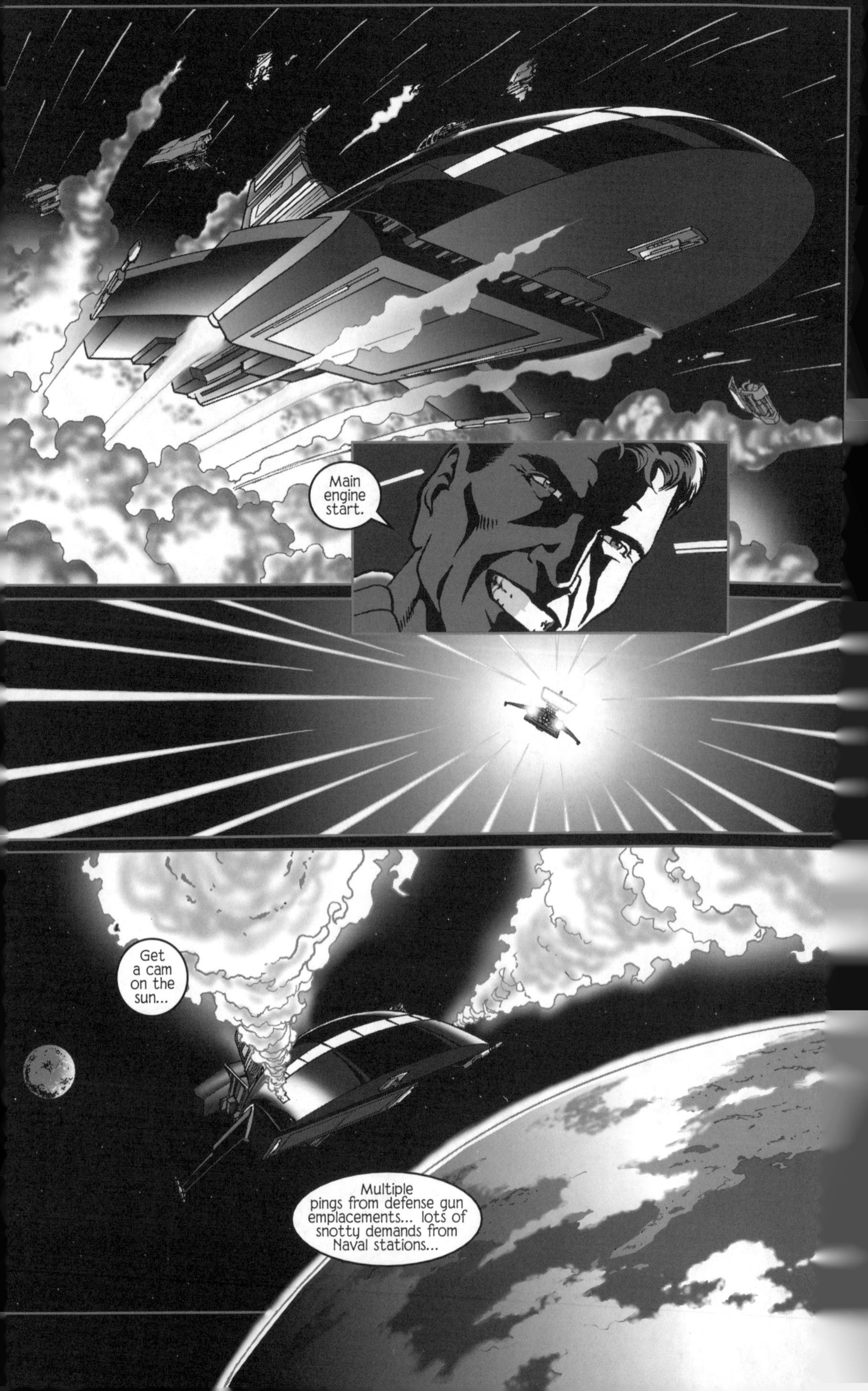
Main engine start.
Get a cam on the sun...
Multiple pings from defense gun emplacements... lots of snotty demands from Naval stations...

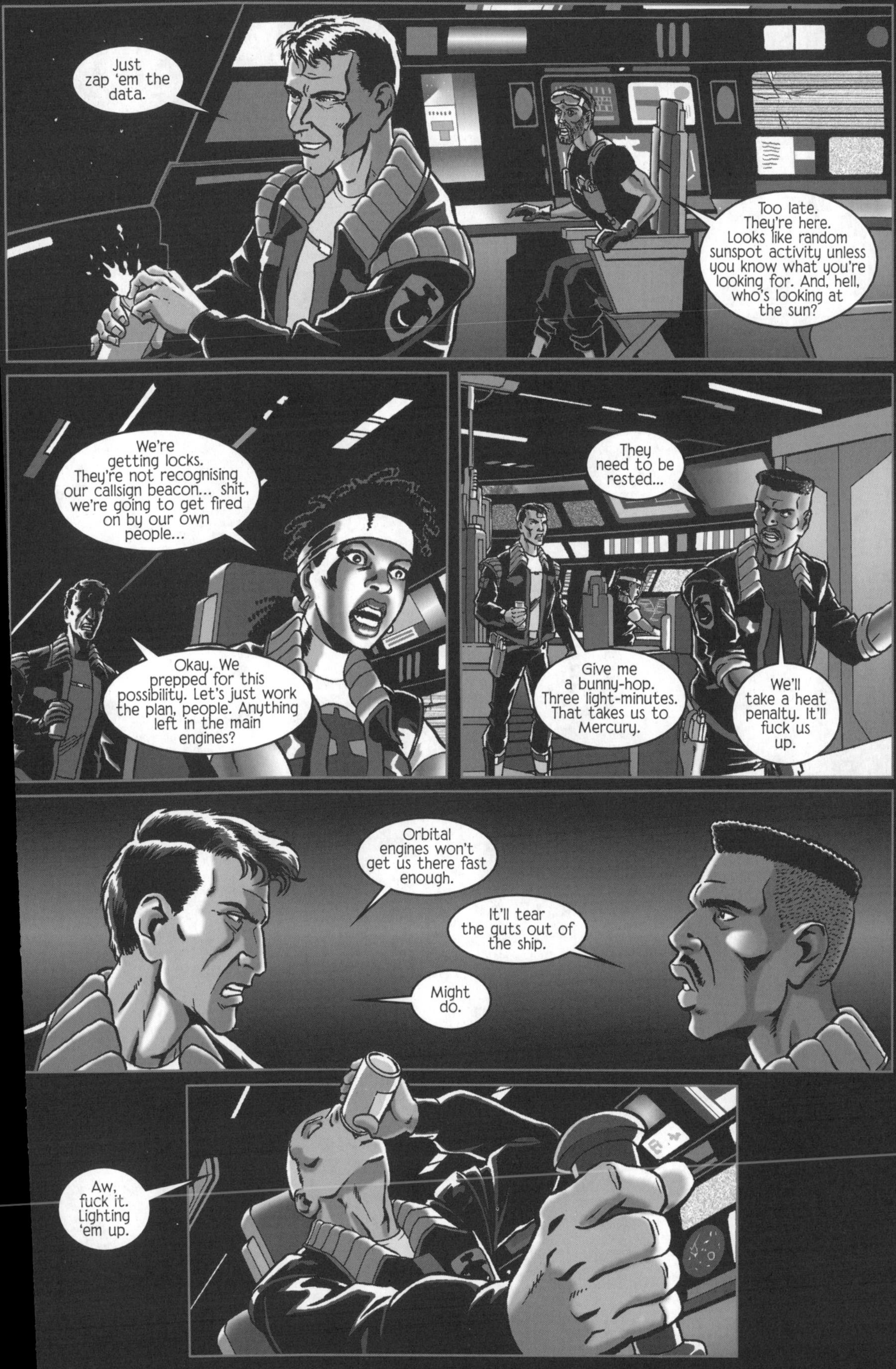
Just zap 'em the data.
Too late. They're here. Looks like random sunspot activity unless you know what you're looking for. And, hell, who's looking at the sun?
We're getting locks. They're not recognising our callsign beacon... shit, we're going to get fired on by our own people...
Okay. We prepped for this possibility. Let's just work the plan, people. Anything left in the main engines?
They need to be rested...
Give me a bunny-hop. Three light-minutes. That takes us to Mercury.
We'll take a heat penalty. It'll fuck us up.
Orbital engines won't get us there fast enough.
It'll tear the guts out of the ship.
Might do.
Aw, fuck it. Lighting 'em up.

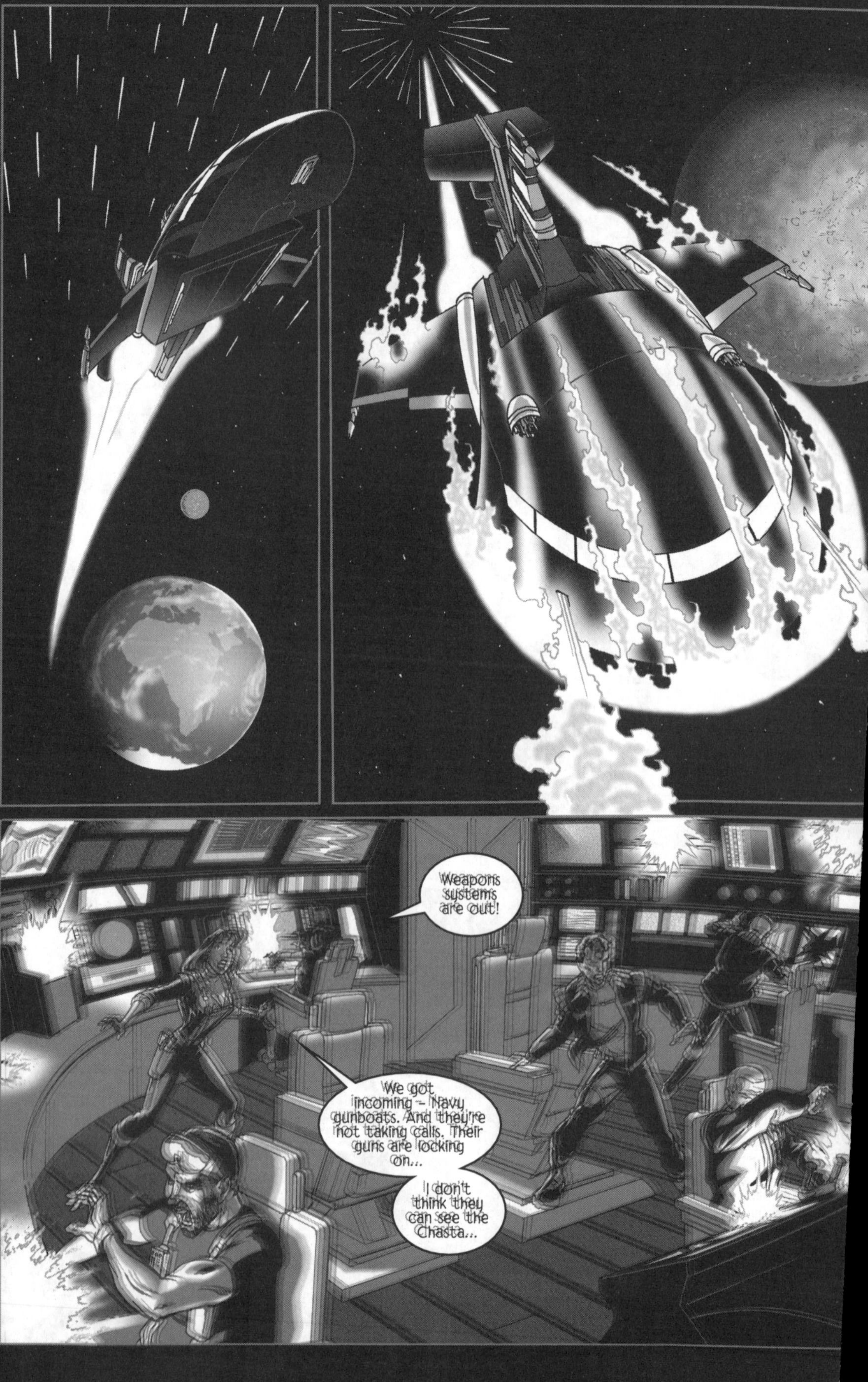
Weapons systems are out!
We got incoming -- Navy gunboats. And they're not taking calls. Their guns are locking on...
I don't think they can see the Chasta...

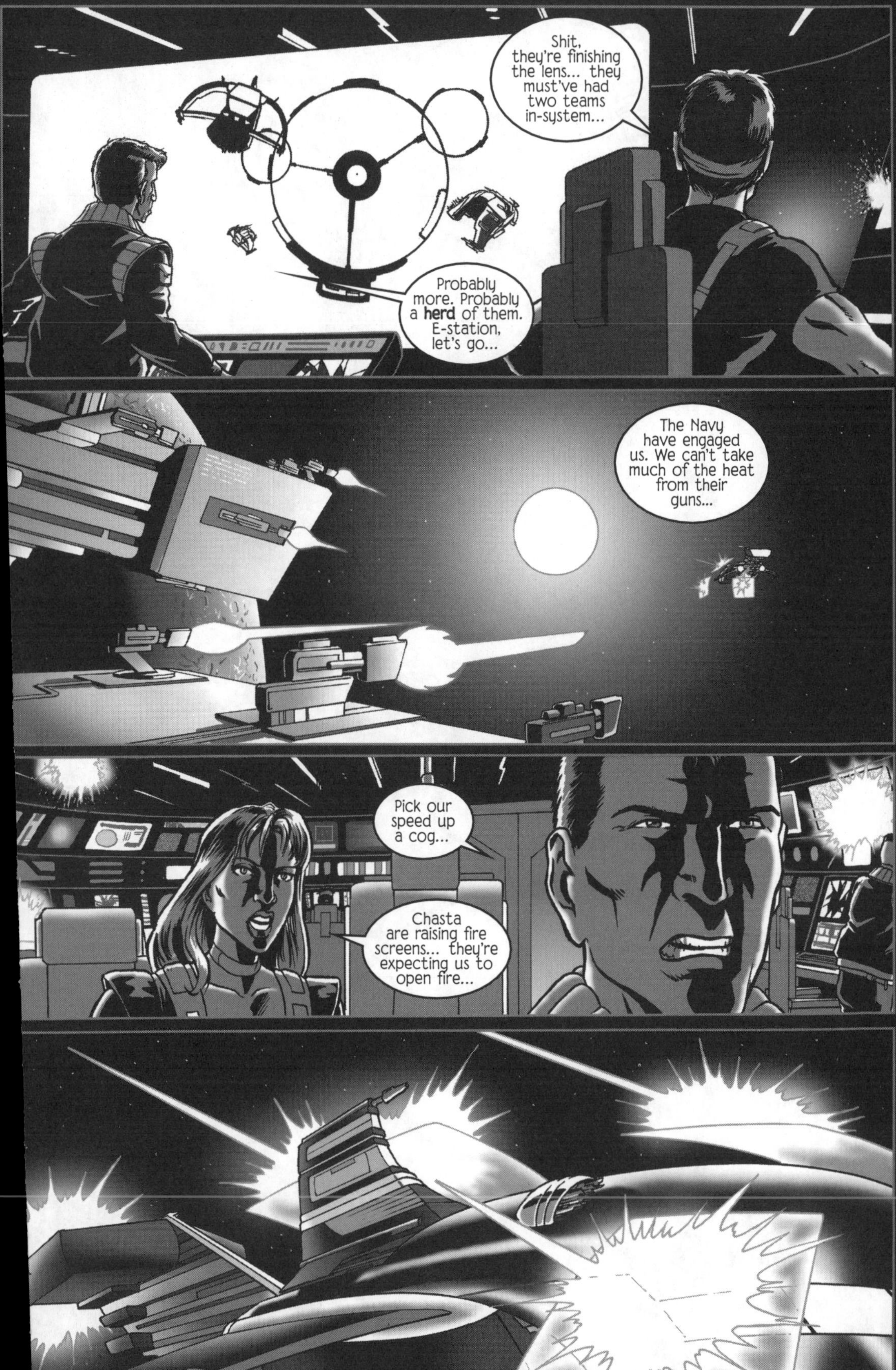
Shit, they're finishing the lens... they must've had two teams in-system...
Probably more. Probably a **herd** of them. E-station, let's go...
The Navy have engaged us. We can't take much of the heat from their guns...
Pick our speed up a cog...
Chasta are raising fire screens... they're expecting us to open fire...

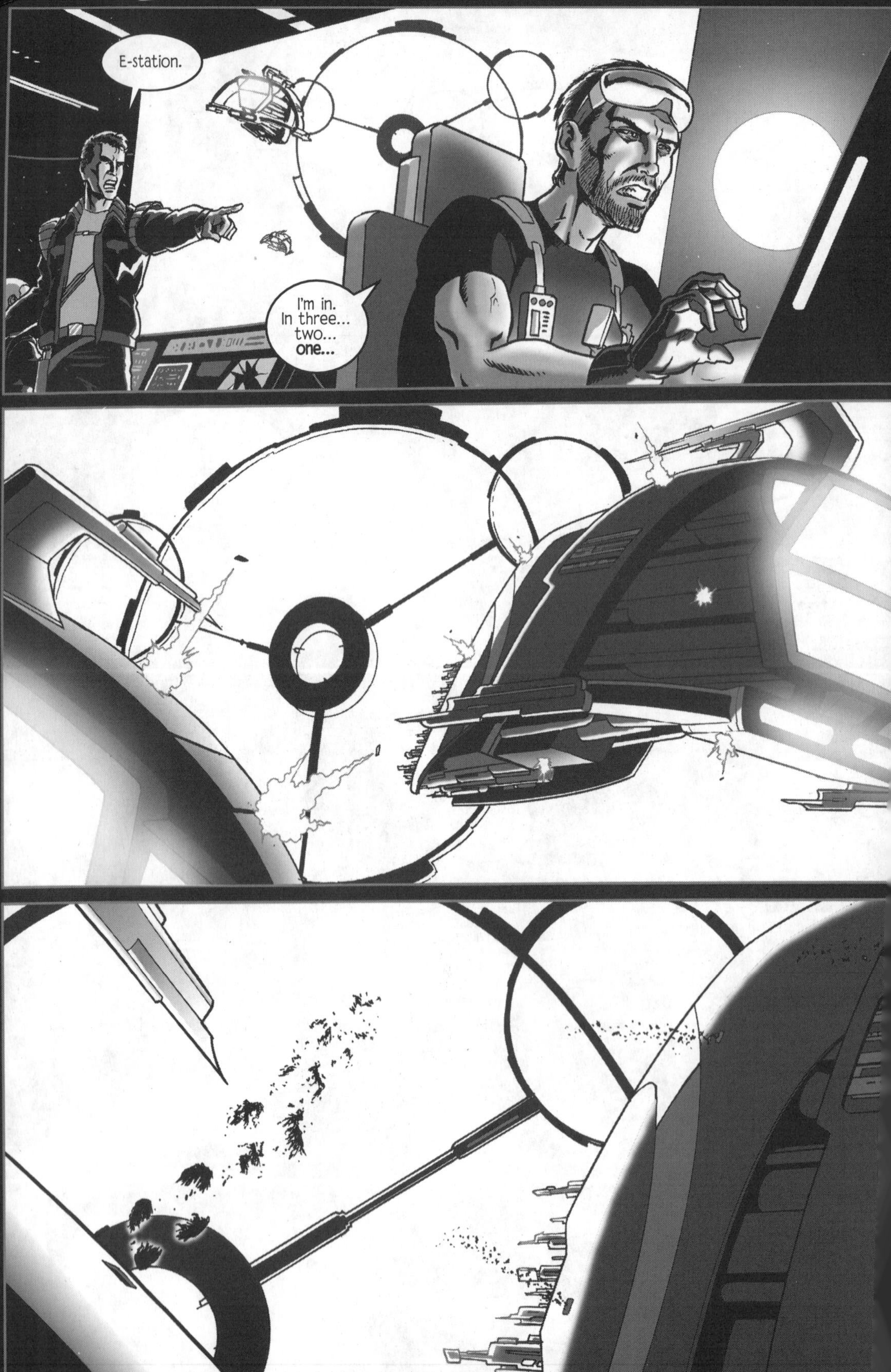
E-station.
I'm in. In three... two... one...

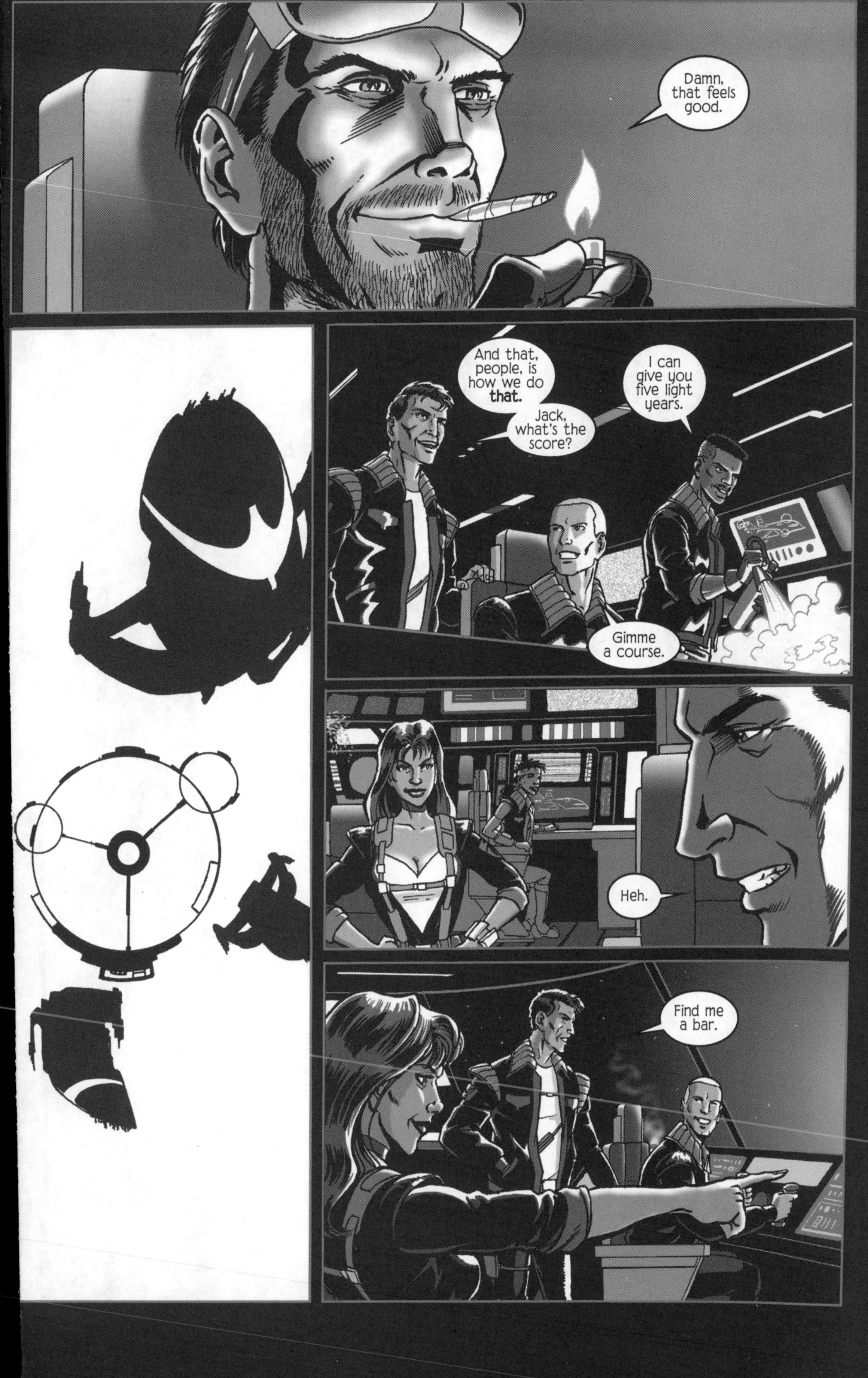

Damn, that feels good.
And that, people, is how we do **that.**
Jack, what's the score?
I can give you five light years.
Gimme a course.
Heh.
Find me a bar.

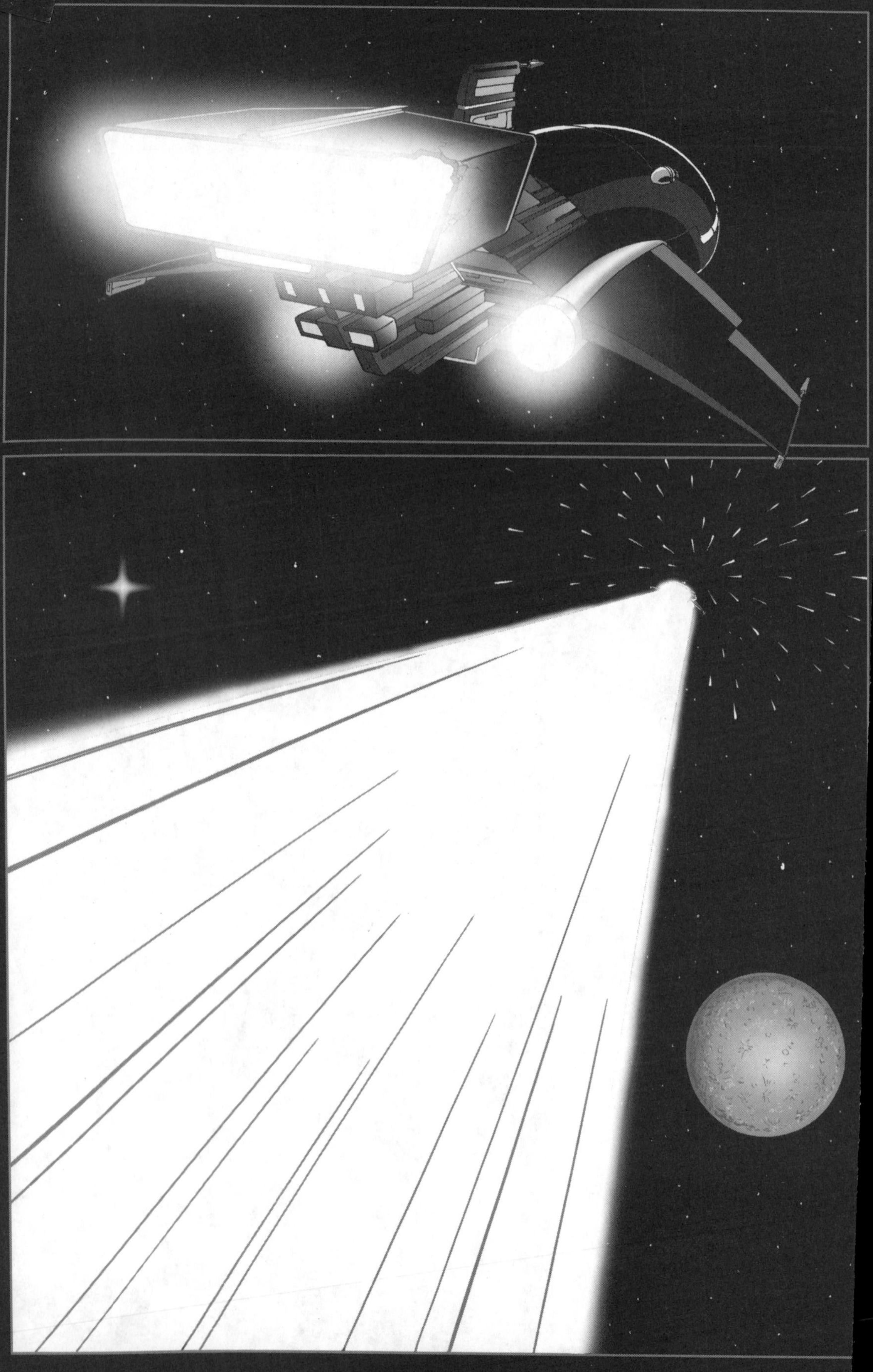